WHOLLY
JESUS

HIS SURPRISING APPROACH TO
WHOLENESS
AND WHY IT MATTERS TODAY

MARK FOREMAN

ampelōn
PUBLISHING
ampelonpublishing.com

To

I dedicate this book to my spiritual mentor, C. S. Lewis, who snuck past my watchful dragons to invade my castle with Aslan's redeeming nature. He taught and modeled for me what it means to be wholly consumed by the Mighty Lion in order to become an agent of wholeness.

CONTENTS

Acknowledgements 6

Foreword by Jon & Tim Foreman 7

0. Inspiring Unintended Moments by Gabe Lyons 13

Part I: Why Wholeness Matters

1. The Whole World Has Gone Whole 19

2. Old Chewing Gum: Wholeness and Salvation 27

3. Pirates, Mutiny and Mutation: How Broken Are We? 41

4. Broken Masterpieces: What Does a Whole Person Look Like? 55

Part II: How Jesus Defined Wholeness

Chapter 5: The Invasion Has Begun 73

Chapter 6: Wholly Jesus in a Material World 91

Chapter 7: Mangers, Mustard Seeds, Children and Crosses 105

Chapter 8: The Wholly Trojan Horse 117

Part III: How Half People Become Whole

Chapter 9: Raising the Bar to Normal 131

Chapter 10: Becoming Spirit People 149

Chapter 11: Risk, Sacrifice and Wholly Transformation 165

Chapter 12: Building a Church Without Walls 187

Chapter 13: Wholeness Will Prevail 205

Notes 221

ACKNOWLEDGEMENTS

For my wonderful wife and friend, Jan, who has shared countless hours and vacation days to allow me to finish this manuscript, I am most grateful. I want to thank my sons, Jon and Tim, for their encouragement and for modeling in the music industry much of what I believe about influencing culture. I am indebted to believers, such as Cassie and Jenny Carstens, Joseph DeSousa, Sameh, Eddie, and others around the world who have modeled transformational Christianity for me. Much thanks to Brent Cole for believing in this project, masterfully editing it and coaching me along the way, and to Jason Chatraw for believing in and publishing this work. And I am grateful for countless friends and loved ones who have believed in this project and, with me, believe that transformed people can transform this world.

FOREWORDS

Immature poets imitate; mature poets steal." Maybe Picasso stole that concept from T. S. Elliot—or maybe neither of 'em said it. Either way my confession is this: I am both a thief and an imitator of my father.

The best parts of me are simply echoes of my dad. He's still showing me patience after all these years—still showing me how to love the folks that insult me. And so the song remains the same: though I'm a few inches taller than my dad, he remains a much bigger man than I.

So you see my predicament in writing this forward: I am the shadow asked to introduce the object who has cast it. I am the cartoon asked to introduce the real thing. To usher in his words with my own could be a bit redundant.

So I shall begin by talking about everything that is not written in this book, the things between the lines, the shadows that only a son can know. The early morning surf sessions at Pipes. The late morning philosophy chats at Swami's. Staring at the stars and talking about how quickly time passes. He was there even during the broken times when nothing was right. My dad, to my amazement, has always been the man who won't try to fix me, just love me.

I am so proud of him. Stories I hear of my dad remind me of other heroes of mine. Stories like the time when he gave his minivan to a band who was broken down on the side of the road; he'd never met them before but they needed a car. Times when he stood strong and tall in the face of opposition. There's a friend of mine who said her main reason for belief in God was knowing my folks. No joke. I know what she means though; we see what God is like in the faces of those around us. And though my dad has his flaws like everyone else, I often see God though him, through the things he says and does. And now, through what he has written.

With the word "wholeness" trapped in the ether of the tabloids, it can be a dangerous thing to write about—particularly risky stuff for a pastor. Yet it was The Teacher himself who was deeply concerned about our entire being. He lived and died that the broken would know wholeness. "For whoever wants to save his life will lose it, but whoever loses his life for me and for the gospel will save it." Blessed are the broken, for they will be made whole.

I have learned so much about this strange, inverse relationship from my dad. I feel like he embodies it better than anyone I know. In some ways this book doesn't do his life justice—it's like a band's studio record that can't quite capture the live experience. Though these pages are quite an album in and of themselves, I've seen the live show all my life.

My father's "music" often came to me in the form of an ongoing dialogue. A few hours ago, I had a conversation with one of the most inspiring musicians I've ever met. He was telling me about a church that had kicked him out, an experience that deeply wounded him. I know what that feels like, to be misunderstood and abused by the folks who are supposed to be loving you—fighting for you. I've had many great conversations with my dad about this. He says the church is like your extended family, crazy second uncles and cousins that might drive you mad. But they are still your family; and they are the only family you'll ever get. You have the privilege of loving them.

Yes, the church is beat-up, ugly, and splintered. Even wrong at times. Tele-evangelists, bigots, hypocrites ... yup. It's easy to take shots at the church. So in the age of American individualism and personal salvation, there is the temptation to disown the whole lot and reinvent the wheel. "We'll start fresh!" And yet to think that we're going to be the first church that gets it right is ludicrous. We're never going to find "Christian wholeness" on our own, not without loving the folks around us.

Yes, the church is broken. It's always been broken. We are a body of misfits, losers, misdirected souls who are desperate for healing. But let the hospital never abandon the sick patients; let the church never abandon the broken. The broken are the bride of Christ—the broken are our family. We, the damaged souls, are the church.

So in this cacophony of brokenness I often look to my dad's words to figure out how to heal. How to grow. How to become more whole. And his words always point me back to The Teacher of wholeness, the only one who can bring peace. The one who came so that we could have whole life, abundant life, and I am thirsty for this life he gives.

In this broken world we face sorrow. We face death and pain. We face the horrors of our own shattered humanity. But our yearning for wholeness is beneath it all; we will be satisfied in God alone. In this longing, I am an immature poet aping God when I try to find wholeness in and of myself. I must continually be reminded to find peace in the Father of the heavens alone.

For this, I'll keep stealing from my dad.

Jon Foreman, *frontman for Switchfoot*

We are a beautiful letdown,
Painfully uncool,
The church of the dropouts
The losers, the sinners, the failures and the fools
Oh what a beautiful let down
Are we salt in the wound
Let us sing one true tune

Words to a song that my brother wrote, a song that we've played hundreds of times, all over the world. And yet, they still resonate deeply within my soul. What a broken people we are. Spending most of my formative years growing up in the laid-back surf culture of north county, San Diego, I am very familiar with the growing search for a remedy. Answers are seemingly found within the bulletin boards, flyers, books, and pamphlets in nearly every storefront shop or cafe. And yet, as the number of remedies increases, ironically so does the demand. There is obviously a large disconnect here.

This observation is not limited to my hometown, however. As a touring musician, I've enjoyed the opportunity to travel throughout the world. I love seeing things from a new vantage point—experiencing other cultures, food, music, waves and everything else along the way. In all these travels it becomes clear that while the desire for wholeness is certainly nothing new, there is a growing global awareness of our brokenness and a newfound urgency towards restoration. Of course, if I'm truly seeking evidence of our innate human need for wholeness, I need look no further than the confines of my own heart.

This is why we sing. Singing allows us safe passage through the treacherous waters of the soul. Our hopes and fears, our doubts and our beliefs—these are frightening caves to explore, and even worse to talk about. But in a song, all matter is fair game. "We are a beautiful letdown ... the church of the dropouts, the losers, the sinners, the failures and the fools." It's an all-too accurate description of humanity when we try to fix ourselves. "Oh what a beautiful letdown... Let us sing one true tune!" For me, the letdown is the painful reality that no matter how hard I try, I am quite unable to fix myself. I am in desperate need of a savior. But what a beautiful truth. There is such freedom in our surrender to Wholly Jesus, who's offer to us is nothing less than complete wholeness. This is the Beautiful Letdown.

* * *

When my Dad asked Jon and I to write a response to his book, it made me smile. I play rock and roll for a living. What could I possibly say to add to the well-chosen words of my Dad, one of my greatest heroes. Definitely a tall order. My Dad has, without a doubt, played a huge role in shaping who I am and the worldview that I carry. This is the guy who pulled the car over when we heard U2's "Still haven't found what I'm looking for" on the radio for the first time. This is the Dad who introduced me to the magical worlds of Tolkien, Lewis, and MacDonald. The guy who pushed me into my first wave on a surfboard, and the guy who taught me how to play Zeppelin and the Beatles. But perhaps larger than all of these influences, I'm thankful that he allowed me the freedom to explore, make mistakes, dream big dreams, and ask even bigger questions.

No question was ever too big or too small—no dialogue was off-limits. I knew that my Dad's God was a big God, one who wasn't intimidated by my doubts, my questions, my music or my hairstyle. None of these were frightening to the God he knew (although I'm sure some of my hairstyles should have been). But it gets better. Not only was God Almighty not scared by my music, doubts or questions—He was interested in them. He actually wanted to hear that warbly, pre-pubescent imitation of Robert Plant singing Stairway to Heaven. This is the Jesus I was introduced to as a kid: a Wholly Jesus, fully integrated with all aspects of life, culture and even the darkest aspects of my soul.

* * *

I remember one Sunday message in particular that my Dad taught, titled, "No Thin Jesus." The title really sums it up. There is nowhere I can go that is beyond the reaches of redemption. There is no music venue, no song, no lyric that is outside the sphere of this Wholly Jesus. When we started this band called Switchfoot, this is why we saw no disconnect between playing our songs in a bar or in a church.

These were honest songs about hope, doubt, failure and redemption: the broken human condition and the universal longing to be whole. These were songs that needed to be sung in bars, coffee shops, colleges, churches and everywhere else.

They needed to be sung because Jesus' invasion of wholeness is passionate and robust, desiring to integrate all aspects of humanity with himself. So the question that now remains is this: "Where are you gonna go? Salvation is here!"

Tim Foreman, *bassist for Switchfoot*

chapter zero

Inspiring Unintended Moments

I can't imagine a more credible person than Mark Foreman to write the definitive book on holistic Christianity. You'll better understand why when you know how I was introduced to him.

It is a more profound moment than I would ever expect, sitting on our living room couch on a Sunday evening, watching the fall premier of the most popular television show of the season, *Extreme Makeover Home Edition*. As the episode began, host Ty Pennington introduced the Wofford family to the world—a recently widowed father and his eight children in desperate need of hope and better living space.

Anyone who has watched this Emmy award-winning show knows what happens next. The show begins its transition from tragedy to triumph as Ty and his design team set out to rally a mass of volunteers in the community to help in the weeklong demolition and remodeling of a house—in this case, the Wofford's house.

It is hard to picture now but early in the life of *Extreme Makeover Home Edition*, recruiting volunteers wasn't so easy. For this particular episode, it was further complicated by the location—north county San Diego—a vacation haven and a hub of beach lifestyles. Can you imagine the challenge of convincing hundreds to leave the balmy comforts of the ocean breeze and warm sand to help build a home for complete strangers? Enter into the equation North Coast Calvary Chapel, Carlsbad, CA.

Back from commercial break, the shot cuts to Ty Pennington occupying the North Coast pulpit on a Sunday morning. He passionately makes his appeal for electricians, framers, landscapers, painters and anyone able enough to participate. Hundreds of churchgoers jump to their feet and raise their hands. Ty tosses blue volunteer t-shirts from stage as member after member stands to commit a week of their life, and in many cases, personal vacation time to the cause.

I was blown away. Completely encouraged and thrilled to know that a church would rise to the occasion when confronted with the need of a family in its community. And rise up they did, helping create an incredible home and new way of life for this beautiful family.

The pastor of that church is Mark Foreman.

People like Mark do not look for the spotlight—you'd have a hard time finding them taking up the "talking head" spot on national TV—but their stories always seem to make it out, usually unintentionally. They don't care about promoting themselves or their organizations; instead they focus on living an exemplary life and humbly encourage those closest to follow. Their lives reflect the nature of Jesus more than any mission statement ever could and the fruit of their lives is a more compelling lesson than any sermon. And that is why this book has impacted me most. It embodies a life well-lived.

Mark has had numerous opportunities to write a book—but chose not too until now. His foremost commitment was always to have something valuable to add to the conversation. *Wholly Jesus* has surpassed that mark.

In a time when the vast majority of Americans are warm to spirituality, seeking transcendence and longing for answers to life's age-old questions, most of us have come up short. The common expression of Christianity most encounter leaves them wanting or, worse yet, driven to find alternative answers in half-truth pursuits of spiritual fulfillment.

Somewhere along the way, the movement of Jesus got off course. Historically recognized for motivating the fight for justice, community involvement, civil society, volunteerism, justice, freedom for all humankind and a life connected with the rhythms of God's creation— Christianity has now become a label to be scorned. Context is everything and in this challenging cultural environment, Mark Foreman gives a clarion call to Christ's followers to become reacquainted with the core message of the Gospel—that Christ's redemptive work not only offers salvation to the lost but equally compels us to transform all things within our grasp. We really do have good news to share and it centers on this message of wholeness for all of creation.

Mark's approach runs refreshingly counter to attempts by others to hijack Jesus and use Christianity as a religious facade to hide their harsh and mean-spirited prejudices. In stark contrast, he motivates thoughtful engagement in our world by painting a picture that leaves you wondering how it's conceivable you had never thought of the Christian faith in this way.

For those who care about embodying a sincere faith that is loving, authentic, humble and full of grace, *Wholly Jesus* will spur you on. You will be challenged to go deeper into the heart of Jesus and discover for yourself why his message has resonated throughout every generation for centuries. But it won't be enough to recognize it—you will be challenged to embody it. To pursue the kind of life that remains true to the call of Jesus, stimulates questions, invites thoughtful discussion and refreshes a world of unimpressed onlookers.

***

In case you are wondering, at the conclusion of the episode of *Extreme Makeover Home Edition*, it was obvious. Mark and North Coast Calvary Chapel had not only restored a home and the lives of its nine occupants, they had redeemed the reputation of the church. If only for a few minutes, millions saw the Bride of Christ love their neighbor, not just with words but in deeds. It was a beautiful, unintentional, transcendent moment.

My hope is that the valuable time you invest in reading *Wholly Jesus* inspires many more of these unintended moments; that followers of Christ would recover the way of Jesus in their everyday circumstances, relationships, neighborhoods and communities; and that the watching world would be compelled to understand why.

In *Wholly Jesus* we are privileged to discover the impetus behind the well-lived life of my friend and mentor, Mark Foreman. In this discovery, lets remember that to whom much is given, much is required.

Gabe Lyons
Co-Author, *UnChristian*
Founder, Fermi Project and Q

PART I:

WHY WHOLENESS MATTERS

chapter one

The Whole World Has Gone Whole

Many men go fishing all of their lives without knowing that it is not fish they are after.

— Henry David Thoreau

Between the surf communities of Carlsbad and Solana Beach, a lush garden spreads out atop oceanfront cliffs. Its northern gate opens to a meandering brick and flagstone path flanked by tropical trees and koi-filled ponds. I arrived at 7:00 AM for my daybreak tradition.

Faded blue-jean light illuminated the Pacific before the sun crowned the eastern horizon behind me. The garden looked empty as far as I could see. Whispering green space, swaying palm umbrellas, trickling brooks and pools—I had my pick of havens. I followed the flagstone path to a favorite spot on the west end; a bench nestled on the edge of a grass island facing a spectacular view of the reefbreak below. Local surfers call the break "Swami's", after the garden's founder and longtime resident, the Swami Paramahansa Yogananda. He penned his renowned 1946 book *The Autobiography of a Yogi* while watching the same ebbs and flows.[1]

Rounding the path's final bend, I approached my familiar perch. It was only then I noticed a grayed, middle-aged man reclining on the bench swallowed by blooming snapdragons. Disappointed, I slid quietly to another bench and watched for him to leave.

Legs outstretched and crossed at the ankles, a plump gold pillow beneath him, the man alternated between closed-eyed meditation and open-eyed trance. Thirty minutes passed like seconds while my eyes ping-ponged between the man and the surfers 100 feet below. Eventually, I realized the only meditating I'd done was on my desire to ride a wave and my need to drink coffee. I pushed myself up, left the garden and walked to the café across the street.

As I waited in line, I read the corkboard's local ads:

Ion Therapy—Living energy medicine

Somatic Life Coaching—You hold the tools necessary
to find the solutions to all your challenges

NATUROPATHIC FAMILY CARE

Living Prana—Enhancing your well-being holistically

Bon—The indigenous practice of Tibet

My turn came and the young lady behind the counter handed me a white cup. I pumped it full of caffeine and headed back to the garden. As I arrived, the middle-aged man was climbing the steps to leave when our eyes met at the garden gate…

* * *

I'd thought a lot about spirituality in that garden, especially lately— about themes for Sundays sermons or topics from recent conversations. Specifically, I'd been thinking about the term wholeness. It weaves its way into a lot of conversations these days. From yoga to Thai chi to meditation and naturopathic medicine, millions of

Westerners are adopting and practicing Eastern philosophies centered on improving the whole person—body, mind and spirit. The café corkboard is Exhibit A. These pursuits represent a deviation from our historical pursuit of wholeness, which focused only on physical and mental treatments, without consideration for the soul.

Eastern-minded wholeness is no short-term fad either. Americans spend an estimated $3 billion a year on yoga alone,[2] and approximately $40 billion a year on naturopathic treatments in general.[3] Wholeness has clearly become a booming industry with no signs of slowing down. Crowds flock to places like the cliff-top meditation garden and its property-mate, the world-renowned Self Realization Fellowship. Every summer, I watch buses spill out wide-eyed visitors wearing hope on their faces. They all hope for the same thing, and it's a hope common to us all.

I decided some time ago that if opportunity presented itself, I would talk to those I met in the garden. Most are wonderful, warm people and their stories are fascinating. Unless they ask, I rarely tell them I'm a pastor. It tends to muddle their perceptions and our subsequent conversation. Instead, I enjoy simply listening and learning from them. I love to hear their hearts speak and understand their deeper desires. The middle-aged man on my favorite bench was no exception. Before he passed, I struck up a conversation.

***

Richard is his name, he said, and he'd been visiting the garden nearly every day for 20 years. I told him it then made sense why he looked so familiar—we must have crossed paths before, I said. He agreed.

We exchanged pleasantries and then I said, "Can I ask you a personal question, Richard?"

"Sure."

"How does coming here help you?"

"Well," he contemplated, "I believe we're all on a path. Our paths are all different and this kind of place isn't for everyone—but this is part of my path."

"What do you mean by path?"

"Well, regardless of how we come to it, I think we're all searching for wholeness, trying to become better people inside and out. I'm
not saying it's the right path for everyone but my path to wholeness
goes through this garden."

* * *

A World Gone Whole

Humans are proud, ambitious and brilliant. But whether or not
we admit it, we are also porous beings, fundamentally shaped by outside forces: people, philosophies, trends, chemicals and the Divine. It
seems we are predisposed to find our identity in something or someone beyond ourselves. "Self-made" is ultimately an illusion. Still, our
culture believes, like Richard, we can fix ourselves.

Visit Barnes & Noble and you'll find an entire aisle dedicated to
the enterprise of "self-help"—a book category that did not exist fifteen years ago. Its enormous appeal epitomizes the colossal trend
toward holistic self-healing. It seems the personal pursuit-of-whole-
ness has become the current American remedy for the spiritual itch
inside us all.

While many begin their pursuit through the physical door—yoga,
Thai chi, acupuncture, etc.—most seek more than better health. Most
also hope to find therapy for their minds and enrichment for their
souls, remedies for greater meaning to their existence: a fuller humanity. If only the Christian church were better at illuminating Jesus' offer.

The Savior offers nothing short of the wholeness and complete
humanity so many seek. But something surprising sets His approach
to wholeness apart. Contrary to every other approach, His does not
hinge on self-help. He went so far as to say we are not capable of making or keeping ourselves whole (if you look around this is fairly apparent). Instead, He tells us it is only through His-Spirit-in-us that
wholeness can be attained—full humanity from indwelling Divinity.

It is a critical consideration that the Christian church has largely
missed the present significance of Jesus' offer. Why amidst a culture
that seeks wholeness so intently—to the tune of $40 billion a year—

do we still offer a shrunken, otherworldly view of salvation rather than speaking of the robust redemption that Jesus spoke of, the salvation that injects restoration into all of life in us and around us now? Isn't this the very thing pop-culture seeks? These are key questions we will address in the coming pages. Their answers are far more significant than establishing personal preference or denominational doctrine. Your understanding of Jesus' offer of wholeness and its relationship to salvation is critical—especially as a Christian.

In fact, with a deeper understanding of Jesus' offer of and approach to wholeness, you might begin to wonder if the infusion of Eastern philosophy into Western pursuits might be something good— even something of a lesson from God. In the very least, the wholeness pursuits of Western pop-culture can remind us of a critical component of Christ's message we've forgotten.

For certain, there are lines that must be drawn as followers of Christ, but there are also lines we've drawn that limit Christ's message. When it comes to the topic of wholeness, it seems we may need an eraser.

On the other hand, there are certainly churches and individuals that recognize the spiritual significance of our culture's fascination with health and wholeness. Still, they are the minority.

Prevailing Christian posture is anti-Eastern philosophy and therefore distrusting (or at least ignorant) of the immense popularity of yoga, Thai chi, acupuncture and naturopathic treatment in general. I know of a few in my church who still sneak to yoga class each week for fear of being cast as heretics. It's a posture we need to clarify and modify according to Scripture. We haven't done this for some time— but if there was ever a time, it is now.

Ultimately, when we clarify Jesus' offer of wholeness and then place it in the context of mainstream spiritual conversation, we find many common threads. Knowing which threads form a tapestry of truth is a major key to presenting people with the redemptive wholeness they crave and need—people like Richard from the garden. It is also a key to knowing what about the prevailing holistic philosophy we should embrace and what we should not.

A WHOLLY POSTURE

While the Apostle Paul waited in Athens for Silas and Timothy to join him, he took stock of the city's culture. He noticed idols everywhere—Athens was the philosophy and spirituality capital of the world at that time and this was evident by the many forms and objects of worship. People everywhere were searching for wholeness and establishing many paths to this end. Paul was immediately burdened for the Athenians and he began approaching Christians and non-Christians alike with Jesus' full offer: He died that we would be restored to wholeness. A group of popular philosophers got wind of Paul's conversations and invited him to Mars Hill where locals hung out and discussed the latest ideas. There, Paul contextualized Jesus' message within the mainstream conversation. He understood what the people ultimately sought—wholeness—and he presented them with a new way to find it. He presented to them not only a Holy Jesus, the perfect sacrifice for the sins of mankind, but also a Wholly Jesus, the remedy for the brokenness of the world.

In many ways, today's modern world is quite similar to the ancient Athens where Paul once stood. And as fellow Christians, we too should recognize that the distinctiveness of Jesus' offer sets Him apart from today's other wholeness remedies. If we overlook this, we quietly remove Jesus from today's mainstream spiritual conversation. We also push people like Richard from the reach of church influence.

***

As we continued our conversation that morning, he talked openly about finding his path to wholeness.

"I grew up in a Presbyterian church," he admitted with some discomfort.

"It wasn't for you?"

"Don't get me wrong. I know that kind of place is where some people need to be. I don't want to leave the impression I'm against Christianity because I'm not. But as I got older I started to realize what I was looking for was life and I wasn't finding it at church. For me, the church was all about dogma. All it wanted to do was argue and be right."

***

I intersect with life-seekers like Richard nearly every week in the garden and nearly everywhere I travel. They are not shy to talk about what they seek. They want better health, a sounder mind and a peaceful soul. They want a wholly life—a more meaningful and complete life—and they look for it where it seems most likely to be found: in Eastern philosophy, in Buddhist temples, in yoga and Thai chi classes and in lush meditation gardens along the southern California coast.

Like Richard, many wholeness-seekers see in the Christian church something churchgoers don't: What we offer is not wholly what Jesus' offered. We have somehow (and quite inadvertently in many cases) reduced His promise of perfect wholeness to "forgiveness for now and hope for later" or to an edgy ad campaign about giving church and God a chance.

The sum of what is seen is that Christians seem to live half-lives (with the Spirit of whole-life in our hearts), and we seem to offer half-life (with the promise of wholeness in our hands). It's a pattern we have to change. That begins when we seek to comprehend Jesus' whole message and then learn to place it in today's dialogue. The combination has eternal implications.

chapter two

Old Chewing Gum:
Wholeness and Salvation

To the man who only has a hammer in the toolkit, every problem looks like a nail.

— Abraham Maslow

"Are you saved?" she asked. My head bent down with my eyes staring at nothing but a sea of shag carpet. I was at a loss, nervously fumbling with my paisley bellbottom cuffs. Though we were friends and spoke the same language, I hadn't a clue what she was asking me. She was so different, now. So somber. What did she mean by *saved*?

Kathy had been gone for months. She'd escaped to San Francisco, but I heard from a friend she was back and had become religious, something about meeting a street-preacher. Now she and I were talking and it was clear she was zealous for something.

"If you were to die tonight," she persisted, "do you know that you'd go to heaven?"

We were sitting cross-legged style in her parents' living room, staring at each other through our long, scraggly hair. We were just 17, but the rapidly changing world of the 1960's was aging us early. JFK's assassination, Vietnam, the Cold War and the growing protests on college campuses seemed to elevate the significance of her question. It did feel like the end of the world. Would I go to heaven? Is that what she meant by saved?

"I-I-I don't know," I stammered, still staring at the ground.

"Are you a Christian?" she asked, striking another blow like a relentless prosecutor.

I grasped the shag and sifted it through my fingers to brave an answer, "I-I think so." I felt a little more confident about that question because even though I was open to other religions I knew I wasn't Buddhist, Hindu, Muslim or Jewish. By process of elimination I must be a Christian.

"Uh-uh," she retorted, wagging her blond head sideways. "If you were, you'd know it."

Stunned and hollow, I climbed into my paneled '62 VW Bus and drove away. All the way home her question pinged in my brain.

***

Forty years this side of her question, I am strangely thankful for her interrogation. It got me thinking. But I now question her skinny definition of the word *saved*. I have grown to believe that getting saved is far more robust than buying insurance for heaven. But for a long time this incomplete understanding of salvation kept me from accepting the wholeness offered by Jesus. It also kept me from including Jesus in all areas of my humanity.

I am not challenging the narrowness of the path. To be certain, Jesus was abundantly clear on this point. But I dispute the all-too-common pop-Western presentation of the gospel—that salvation is *only* or *mainly* about forgiveness and heaven, when in reality, it is much, much more.

There used to be a popular bumper sticker floating around that said, "Christians aren't perfect, just forgiven." The slogan misses the mark, but perhaps for a different reason than you think. It is true that we aren't perfect, and it is true that we are forgiven; but the lie is in the word "just." We are not "just forgiven." We are *forgiven*, but salvation is a whole lot more. And it's the "more" that today's culture so desperately seeks.

OLD CHEWING GUM

Words are like old chewing gum—they lose their flavor after they've been over-jawed. Decades of cultural erosion have a way of morphing and blunting their power. Overused and abused, some terms end up losing the crisp, clarion call of their beginnings. Two words of which this is true are *wholeness* and *salvation*. Both have lost their unique flavor in the mouths of many generations.

The Multi-flavoring of Wholeness

Wholeness has become a bland, umbrella term that is far too general. Like a spinning weathervane, it has no direction, no specificity, no grounding. The result: there is no consensus as to what a fully whole human being looks like or how one gets there. No doubt, wholeness in the mind of the masses still points to the idea of something being repaired or being made complete, but there is little clarity beyond that idea. In an era of relativity it is therefore assumed, "What is whole for you may not be whole for me." Our compass for wholeness has no north, and so the goal, the measure and the means of wholeness vary from person to person.

As an experiment, try telling a few people at an evening party or social gathering that you "don't feel whole," or that you "want to be more whole." Don't go into specifics, just leave it general and then brace yourself for an onslaught of varying advice. Whatever worked for them is the very thing you need. Medicine, vitamins, therapy, acupuncture, chiropractics, religion, books and yoga are suddenly all on the table—an instant buffet of wholeness remedies. You and I get to choose our favorite flavor. To offer wholeness nowadays is like offering someone a beverage, different drinks are suitable at different times. The flavor of wholeness is broad and relative, with no trace of its original distinction. To offer it means nothing and everything at the same time.

The De-flavoring of Salvation

Salvation, on the other hand, suffers from the opposite problem. Once a broad, secular term referring to any occurrence of rescue or liberation in this life, it has dissolved into merely an otherworldly reli-gious term relating to the immaterial soul. Today's salvation refers to getting into heaven or merely "finding religion" and seems unrelated to fixing the physical or emotional realities of life. Following suit, today's flavorless salvation is often presented as one's "real" need, yet seems unrelated to the "perceived" needs of daily life. Perhaps then, it is easy to understand why the word seems so meaningless to the people of our culture who are searching for help, healing and whole-ness now. *Salvation*, like *wholeness*, has also lost its true flavor in the mouths of modern and postmodern conversation.

* * *

Fortunately, when a word melts into complacency, the concept isn't entirely lost. Once upon a time the two terms were bursting with distinct and desirable flavor, and more importantly, they were perfect-ly complementary. If we're to restore them to full flavor in today's cul-ture—and present them as Jesus did—we should return to their ori-gins and then progress from there to Jesus' surprising, but all-encom-passing, definition.

REVIVING THE ANCIENT FLAVOR OF WHOLENESS

Wholeness was initially a robust term, and the pursuit of it was always connected to a combination of physical health, personal moral-ity, religion, and cultural compatibility. Ancient physicians or healers were always concerned with treating the whole person, making little distinction between soul and body, religion and medicine, the individ-ual and society.

In the ancient Middle East, a Babylonian doctor's hand was to be cut off if a simple abscess surgery resulted in the patient's death. An individual's wholeness was considered to be related to the culture's well-being.

An ancient Egyptian papyri discovered in the 19th century relays a long list of remedies with surgical procedures and their correspon-ding spells or incantations. The physiological, medicinal and spiritual were not distinguished.[1]

The Hebrews' contribution will be discussed later on since it was foundational to Christ's definition of wholeness, but suffice it for now to say that the Old Testament hygiene laws were considered profound in matters of public wholeness for the ancient world.[2] However, wholeness for the Hebrews could not be achieved in total without an understanding of their God, Yahweh. Through God's spiritual, ethical and moral direction, the Israelites strove to live integrated lives with those around them and those who lived before and after them. Spiritual wholeness was not distinguished from social wholeness.

Ancient Asia also combined spiritual, philosophical, medicinal and ethical practices to achieve wholeness. In India, the golden age of medicine (800 BC to 1000 AD) was marked by profound medical insight. However, the religious, Hindu view of anatomy influenced their medicine. The Hindus believed the body was made up of three divine universal forces: spirit (air), phlegm, and bile (bodily fluids). Wholeness therefore depended on the balance of these three elementary substances. Hindu physicians used all five senses in diagnosis, and this dependence was matched by their use of magic. Their use of purgatives, sneezing powders, enemas, inhalants, leeches and bleeding were standard. Herbal, animal and mineral remedies were also employed; and because of their strict religious beliefs, hygienic standards were enforced including baths, cleansing oils, eyewashes and the amount of water to be drunk before and after a meal.[3]

Basic, traditional Chinese medicine consisted of the dualistic, cosmic philosophy of the yin and the yang. The yang, the male principle, was active, light and representative of the heavens. The yin, the female principle, was passive, dark and representative of the earth. Wholeness was achieved through a balance of the yin and yang in each person. This philosophy was thus integrated into their medical practices. They believed blood vessels contained blood and air, in proportions depending on the yin and the yang. To treat disease, drugs were used together with herbs and the taking of the pulse to restore the harmony of the yin and yang. Acupuncture was also used to properly distribute the yin and yang throughout the body.[4]

***

Although ancient wholeness philosophies and therapeutic techniques differed from culture to culture, their three commonalties give us a good taste of the original flavor of the word *wholeness*:

1. All ancient cultures sought to achieve wholeness by combining philosophical (mind), medicinal (body) and religious (soul) treatments. Thus the traditional "medicine man" was not only medicinal, but also philosophical and religious in his approach. His work helped compose catalogs of herbs, prognoses of diseases and practices of medicine that proved helpful over the years, some of which are still used today.

2. One's wholeness was seamlessly tied to how one related to God or the gods (spirituality), how one lived toward others (morality) and how one lived in an integrated way with oneself (integrity).

3. Wholeness necessitated an individual being treated as a part of the whole society, rather than as an isolated unit. Individual wholeness was essential to societal wholeness.

In sum, through different techniques all ancient cultures followed a bio-psycho-socio-spiritual model of wholeness: *a model of wholeness that combined the healing of body, mind, soul and culture.* Each element was equally essential and integrated with the others. The elements did not stand alone, but rather held their value in relation to the whole model. Treating only the body or only the mind was unheard of in those days, as was merely pursuing wholeness for the soul. These descriptions were just as true of the Hebrew culture on which Christianity was built. To be *holy* (set apart) did not merely mean being set apart for God in body only, or in soul only. To be *holy* as a Hebrew was to be set apart wholly in body, mind, soul and culture. And that was embodied by loving God with one's whole being.

This is also true of the New Testament Christian. Jesus comes not to serve one part of the person, but the whole person (mind, body and soul), and in so doing, bring redemption to culture. In fact, much of the epistles are embroiled in a defense against what later became Gnosticism: the belief that the physical (the mind and body) was inconsequential and it was only the spiritual (the soul) that God, and therefore we, must focus on. But ancient followers of Christ like the Apostle Paul understood that to be whole meant being mentally, physically, spiritually and culturally well. Unfortunately, we modern followers of Christ seem to have forgotten this ancient understanding. In fact, many outside the church—those seeking wholeness whole-heartedly, like Richard in the garden—seem to hold a better grasp.

Still, today's inconsistent understanding of wholeness falls well short of the full meaning it once held. Today, wholeness is primarily known as a popular self-help term with various manifestations. If commercialized, it would be available in vending machines in many shapes, sizes and flavors. Depending on the user, wholeness can have a psychological, medical, spiritual or nutritional emphasis. Sometimes it has an Eastern philosophical tilt (Yoga, Thai chi, acupuncture ...) while at other times it appears to be grounded in modern Western science (pharmacology, physical therapy, psychology, etc.). The term is so broad today that it can mean whatever the presenter wants it to mean. It might be limited to a specific field of wellbeing or include everything under the sun. As the earlier social experiment demonstrated, when we say "wholeness," there is no consensus of understanding like the ancient cultures had, and this poses a major quandary.

In Search of a True Authority

In ancient times only the religious authorities or medicine men could define the meaning of wholeness. They were the holy guides to wholeness. In modernity (the Enlightenment period between the 17th century to the latter part of the 20th century), the medical doctor was primarily authorized to define it. Now, in this postmodern era, the individual is the primary authority. We are both the patient and the practitioner of wholeness, applying whatever remedy seems best to us. We, the sick, are authorized to give our own prognosis, which includes mixing and matching remedies to our heart's content. In so many words, we assert: "I will tell myself the definition of wholeness, when I will be whole and by what means I will become whole." We are the wizard's apprentice left alone in the laboratory to experiment with anything and everything.

Today's autonomous attitude towards wholeness, however frightening, is here to stay so there is no point in attempting to reverse the
clock. With the Internet at our beckoning, medical and therapeutic
information has become accessible to everyone. And in many ways it
is quite beneficial. We the consumer are empowered, leading us to
become more active in our journey toward wholeness. But without a
clear and common target, we aim at anything and the wholeness bulls-
eye moves with each passing fad.

We subsequently ignore critical questions like: *What is wholeness?*
Who is whole? Who decides when we get there? Like a ship without a
course or a compass, we venture out for the ultimate destination with
only a trial-and-error strategy. We try this vitamin, that yoga or the
other therapeutic treatment. We talk to each other to find out what
someone else has tried and what route seems most promising. We
hope, eventually, the wind and waves will point us on the perfect
course. Unfortunately, this sea before us is immense and confusion
abounds. We're more likely to drift into a perfect storm than a safe
harbor. What we need is a trustworthy captain and a reliable compass.

It is fine, even beneficial, for us to construct disciplines specializ-
ing in particular aspects of wholeness. Today we have one focused on
the physical (medicine, physical therapy and nutrition), another
focused on the mind, emotions and how we think (psychology),
another focused on relationships (marriage and family therapy) and
others focused on society (social workers, courtrooms, non-profits
and so on). But it is an insufficient and ultimately doomed strategy to
only focus on bodies, emotions, relationships or societies. Our pursuit
is doomed without any spiritual and ethical centeredness. Ironically,
our quest for wholeness is at risk of becoming increasingly un-whole.

The honest seeker of wholeness must eventually discover what the
ancients in every culture understood to be paramount: spiritual and
social standards have always been the magnetic north of any pursuit
of wellbeing. Goodness, love, truth, beauty and justice were always
the centerpiece of the pursuit of wholeness. It is with this foundational authority that we must reconstruct a true definition of wholeness.
The remaining chapters will tackle this challenge. This process can

only begin by retrofitting our understanding of salvation—the once primary catalyst in the pursuit of true wholeness. Reconstructing the full meaning of salvation will provide us with the map, compass and captain for our ultimate journey.

REVIVING THE ANCIENT FLAVOR OF SALVATION

When we return salvation to its original flavor, we will find that it and wholeness were once inextricably connected. It might be said that salvation was once the door to the wholeness.

Salvation historically had a wide-range of application to mean *deliverance, liberation, to be rescued,* or *recovered.* A "savior" of an individual or a society was a protector, deliverer or liberator who rescued people from a plight, disease or bondage. He was one who ushered wholeness—of the mind, body, soul and culture—to the people.

There is a reason the name Jesus is always associated with the word *savior.* The root of the Hebrew word for *salvation* is *ysa*, from which the name *Jesus* is derived. The verb *ysa* means *to be roomy*, with the idea that deliverance makes things more spacious, more freeing. It also indicates that without salvation we are bound, confined, narrow and imprisoned. Psalm 103:3-6 describes the salvation Jesus offered to include forgiveness, healing, fulfillment and justice.

When John the Baptist's father, Zechariah, prophesies about the coming Messiah in Luke 1:67-80, he describes the salvation he brings with a word picture from the Old Testament familiar to the Jews of his time: *the horn of salvation*. The picture arose from a society of shepherds who often witnessed a bull or ram raising their horns to do battle and achieve victory. Ancient armies frequently used the same horns to call troops to battle. The phrase speaks of the strength and thoroughness of the salvation the Messiah can bring. It is no meager salvation. It includes the personal display of God's love, the fulfillment of his promises, his rescuing us from our enemies, his transforming our character to serve God and others, and his giving hope and emotional healing, peace (wholeness and wisdom in living) and forgiveness. And this salvation of which Zechariah speaks is primarily in this world, not simply otherworldly. This is a critical point. It seems that throughout history, we have only understood a half-salvation.

The Jews of Jesus' day made the opposite mistake of many Western believers today. First century Jews limited messianic salvation to present military, societal and political deliverance, whereas many 20th and 21st century believers have limited salvation to a future hope and deliverance. Where Jesus' ministry surprises both groups is that it is filled with present tense salvation (forgiveness of present sins, healing, provision, right living, loving relationships and answers to prayer) as well as future tense salvation (forgiveness of future sins, hope, justice and eternal life).

The Lord's Prayer is a simple illustration of the full scope of the Savior's salvation. Jesus prays, "*Your kingdom come* (present tense), *Your will be done on earth* (present tense), *as it is in heaven. Give us today* (present tense), *our daily bread, and forgive us our sins* (present and future tense), *as we forgive those who sin against us* (make past and present relationships whole), *and deliver us from evil* (protect us in the present tense).

All of these requests given by Jesus for his followers to pray involve the salvation that he offers to us in the present tense as well as in the future tense.

The original Greek word for salvation is *sozo*, which means *to rescue or preserve from natural dangers like death, disease and disasters*. To be sure, Jesus' *sozo* in the New Testament takes on the definition of being saved from sin and saved to eternal life. But the *sozo* of Jesus is also used in reference to his rescuing of the disciples and Peter from drowning (Mat 8:25; 14:30); it is used often in reference to the healings of Jesus, 18 times to be exact. Although Jesus' salvation clearly extends to more than just the physical sphere, it is not to the neglect of the physical realm. And the word is not used merely in reference to restoring individuals to wholeness, but also to restoring society and the world to wholeness (John 3:17). Jesus' salvation unto wholeness is for Greeks and Jews, believers and unbelievers, religious and unreligous.

Furthermore, the original flavor of the word *salvation* is not limited to the past or future tenses: *saved, or shall be saved*. It is critical to note the word used in Scripture is in the present tense, *are being saved*.

Christians are often content to use the phrase, "I'm saved," and occasionally the future tense, "will be saved." But we rarely refer to the act of "being saved" in this life. We understand the bookends of our salvation without comprehending the volumes of truth in Scripture regarding "being saved" in this life. It has not always been so.

It wasn't until the early Jews and then the early Christians used the term *salvation* in relation to the Messiah that the word became a primarily religious term. Once *salvation* became parochial in its use, its meaning continued to narrow along the lines of popular religion.

But originally *salvation* was a broad term that:
- Referred to the provision of various needs.
- Referred to the rescuing from various types of disasters.
- Included physical rescue and restoration as well as spiritual (redemption and heaven) and ethical (forgiveness and sanctification) redemption.
- Included the rescue and restoration of societies, not just individuals.[5]

Today, the term has become so restricted in popular Christian circles that it is narrowly equated with forgiveness and real estate in heaven. It has lost the broad definition that Jesus intended in his announcement of the Kingdom of God. Heaven and forgiveness are quite important to be sure; but the vastness of Jesus' offer of salvation-unto-wholeness has been all but lost and this has tremendous implications for personal and social transformation. Especially when it comes to how we, the church, present his offer.

How Jesus feels about the sick and handicapped in this life is often left unexpressed. How Jesus cares about those emotionally distraught, the depressed, those with phobias and addictions, is often left unexpressed. How Jesus cares about the socially oppressed is often left unexpressed. This narrowness also drastically affects how each one of us relates to Jesus and how we represent him to our neighbors.

In the current Western definition of salvation, Jesus is largely limited to the heart. This is not true of the largest portion of believers outside the Western world. But stereotypically speaking, when a Western-minded child is asked, "Where does Jesus live?" the expected answers is, "In my heart." This is all well and good if the child grows up to understand Jesus also lives through my words, my actions, my attitudes, my fantasies, my goals, my finances, my relationships, etc. But sadly, for many Jesus never makes it out of their hearts. He stays inside while the person passively waits for heaven.

One only has to consider the approach Jesus took in addressing the needs of people to properly understand the full meaning of Jesus' offer of salvation-unto-wholeness. He listened, fed, healed, cast out demons, cared for the poor and forgave sins. The number of healings speaks for itself. Furthermore, he confirmed to John the Baptist his mission in Luke 7:22: "So [Jesus] replied to the messengers, 'Go back and report to John what you have seen and heard: The blind receive sight, the lame walk, those who have leprosy are cured, the deaf hear, the dead are raised, and the good news is preached to the poor.'"

Salvation understood from Wholly Jesus' perspective reverses the direction of popular evangelism. Rather than offering to get people into heaven with the real results to come later, Jesus' offer concerns itself primarily with getting heaven into people and thus transforming culture now. He came to invade the lives of broken people and, through them, transform a broken world. This is nothing we must wait for. Wholly Jesus' arrow of salvation is pointing downward from heaven and outward into culture, not inward then upward. (Perhaps it is more appropriate to say followers of Christ are "down and out" rather than "in and up.") Jesus called this invasion "the kingdom of God."

Those his invasion saves are promised heaven but the transformation-unto-wholeness that takes place is defined by the "saved" becoming his agents of further personal and social transformation in this world, not the next.

FROM HERE FORWARD

The two terms, *salvation* and *wholeness,* help the other find its roots. Salvation is the act of restoring unto wholeness. Salvation is the action; wholeness is the product. Together, they represent the process of bringing about a wholly integrated human being. This was and still is Jesus' offer. His salvation-unto-wholeness does not ignore this plan-

et nor despise our humanity; it honors and redeems its original potential. This is why the words *holy* and *whole* are etymologically and con-
ceptually connected. Holy Jesus is Wholly Jesus. Holiness is the manifestation of wholeness.

My desire from here forward is to apply Jesus' offer of *salvation-
unto-wholeness* as he intended, through his message of the kingdom of
God. Sadly, the Western church has often shortchanged itself and the
world in its evangel, and the postmodern influence has hindered its
followers from discovering a remedy for wholeness—one unlike any
other—that leads to an ever-moving transformation of lives and cultures.

***

When Jesus approached the man by the pool of Bethesda, he
asked him, "Do you want to be made well?" He did not ask the man
if he wanted to be *saved*. What did Jesus have in mind? When the man
responded yes, Jesus healed this invalid of 38 years of suffering. This
is the Jesus for which the world is looking.

Throughout the pages of ancient mythology are stories of frogs
becoming princes and princes becoming dragons. This arch-type of
metamorphosis seems to be deeply embedded in the psyche of human
beings. However, it is profoundly significant that Jesus and his gospel
do not describe saved humans becoming angels or spirits or something entirely otherworldly. They describe humans becoming fully
human and reaching their potential. We are called the "new man," a
"new race" and a "new creation." Jesus' offer of salvation-unto-
wholeness is an offer to become fully human. An offer to become the
person you are meant to be in this life and the next.

This offer is profound when you compare how many people woke
today wondering about forgiveness and eternal life versus how many
people woke today wondering about the best way to fix their lives.
The simple point is this: If the Christian church pivots only on people
seeking forgiveness and heaven, then very few will discover the wholeness remedy Jesus offers. However, if we take Jesus' wholly approach,
many will discover what they seek, and more. And many will always
be seeking because we are broken in so many ways.

chapter three

Pirates, Mutiny and Mutations:
How Broken Are We?

Our generation is realistic, for we have come to know man as he really is. After all, man is that being who invented the gas chambers of Auschwitz; however, he is also that being who entered those gas chambers upright, with the Lord's Prayer or the Shema Yisrael on his lips.

— Victor Frankl

I sit alone exhausted, journaling in a dimly lit five-dollar-a-night room in Poipet, Cambodia. I just spent a rigorous, dusty, roller-coaster-day witnessing the darkest corners of human existence and basking in the hopeful laughter of children on a new orphanage playground.

I wandered dark, muddy isles lined with broken shacks on stilts. Poor, huddled faces stared at my clean, foreign face. In respect, I folded my hands and bowed. They watched as their children, scabs on their faces and green mucus hanging from their noses, showed me their pet crab just pulled from the wetlands. They are the second-generation victims of Pol Pot's wicked regime. They are brokenness personified.

Later that day, I played with children who learn in a protected classroom with a warm meal in their stomach and laughter in their voices. They are beauty personified, courtesy of two people, Rose and

Chomno. The two have separately given their lives to feeding, treating, educating, housing and loving Khmer orphans and also adult victims of AIDS. They unapologetically follow and teach the children the ways of Jesus. Being with such heroes causes me a sigh of hope for the human race. All the while, I am fully aware that new Pol Pots are already being raised elsewhere.

The next day I eat dinner across from Chomno, a man usually full of joy. But tonight Chomno's tears spill into his soup as he tells me his tragic, childhood story. It is a poignant reminder that the dark side of humans is never far away. War-greed-refugees-disease-poverty-orphans seems to describe the lifecycle for much of our planet. And it's always the feeble and the children who are most vulnerable.

As a young child Chomno was taken from his parents to work as a slave for the soldiers of Pol Pot. At eight he was forced to labor in the fields for 14 hours a day. With only one watery bowl of soup a day, containing just a few lonely grains of rice, he watched many of his peers die from malnutrition and disease. For four years he served the Khmer thugs, barely escaping death many times. The weak, the sick, the infants and the elderly were regularly executed. The Khmer Rouge needed no reason. They were lawless pirates with power to display.

Chomno fled to Thailand with hundreds of thousands of others when Vietnam invaded Cambodia. There he found refuge in a Buddhist monastery and survived for years by begging on the streets to bring his share of income to the monastery. At 17, he was given an ultimatum: become a monk or move out. Having nowhere to go, he resolved to the monastic life. And then he met a follower of Jesus that very same week. The monastery had taught him there were many ways to follow Buddha. He assumed Jesus to be one of those paths, but when he told his superior about his encounter, Chomno again found himself alone on the streets. He lost everything but his faith.

Now 44, Chomno still follows Jesus, doing the things Jesus did on earth and the same things that had not been done for him: feeding the poor, healing the sick, rescuing girls from human trafficking, schooling the children and teaching their parents. He dreams aloud of a new Cambodia and works tirelessly to tangibly share Jesus' love with the Khmer people. They have been raped of their culture and constantly search of food, health and meaning. The Khmer are a broken people, physically ill and socially impoverished. They have been emotionally and mentally savaged; their families destroyed and displaced; their ancient culture pillaged. Spiritually, they drift without meaning or morals. The devil himself could not have done a better job to shatter their humanity.

THE PARADOX OF US

The pages of human history are filled with blood, war, hatred, death and pain. Yet, stories of ordinary people doing the extraordinary also abound during such times of darkness. In the heart of impoverished Cambodia, people like Rose and Chomno rise up and shine. They exist all over the world—they exist in each of us. In the darkest hours of humanity, heroes still risk their lives to save strangers. Within each of us seems to co-exist the potential to become a Pol Pot as well as a Chomno. We are a paradox indeed; we each possess the potential to become a pirate or a saint.

Stories of heroism reach into our souls because we are all too familiar with the dark side of humanity. War, crime, child abuse and calloused behavior are sadly common. We all wish love made the world go round but when we do look around, we can see there is perhaps a better case for envy, jealousy, hatred and adultery spinning the world so furiously. Sure, we want to trust and to love—but we find it ever challenging because we believe others possess the same paradoxical potential for good and evil. We desire wholeness in all things, but that desire assumes current brokenness. Yes, our desire for integration actually presumes disintegration. We who were made to be whole are ironically dying to live. This begs the questions: Just how broken are we?

By all accounts, we are broken in many ways.

We are ... **Physically Broken.** I'm trying to be patient in a doctor's office while waiting to be seen for three distinct ailments: a sinus infection, a torn meniscus and pre-cancerous spots on my head. I glance down at a *Reader's Digest* lying in the usual magazine cluster. The cover reads, *Trick Your Body Into Staying Young.* Desperate, hopeful and naïve, I tear through the puny magazine till I find page

154. There I discover that the primary "trick" to staying young is having healthy genes, eating right, exercising and staying free of stress. Genetics, stress, exercise and good food ... that's it? No secret? Same old, same old? I suppose I better start listening. After these many miles, my wheels are starting to fall off.

Perhaps the most obvious manifestation of our brokenness—of which I am increasingly aware—is our physical mortality. We die. We are vulnerable creatures susceptible to viral and bacterial infections. We are born with genetic imperfections, built-in design-flaws that prevent us from experiencing our full humanity on a physical level.

Yet, we all desire to be healthy, to live longer. And many see this notion differently. Some aim primarily to be prettier ... skinnier ... more noticed. In the 21st century, rising physical standards have initiated a faulty understanding of wholeness. We often confuse beauty for wholeness in the physical sense. Many trade their lives for this false wholeness but end up merely healthy looking while their actual health continues to diminish. Consider the surprisingly high percentage of smokers in the modeling and acting industries—two segments of society many consult to define health and beauty.

Yet regardless of how we elevate and measure up to society's physical standards, from the age of approximately 30, we gradually begin to age, breakdown and die. We see it in our grey hairs and gravity's effect on our skin. While we can augment our bodies to give the appearance of a younger, healthier person, our flexibility, strength and memory gradually diminish no matter how often we nip, tuck, tan or color.

As if the obvious signs weren't enough, recent research has uncovered the profound depth to our physical brokenness. The mapping of the genome has enabled medical scientists to begin to pinpoint many of the causes of our genetic disorders. But many cures remain only hopeful at best. We now know we are broken at the most microscopic level.

While medical science certainly gives reason for hope and increased longevity, our physical brokenness is inescapable. There is even a downside to living longer that didn't exist when humanity lived shorter lives. With older age comes an increasing prevalence of chronic diseases and conditions that centuries ago, people never faced. Some of these, like Alzheimer's, are nothing short of tragic.

It is this physiological frailty that we despise more than anything and therefore aim to fix more readily than any other arena of brokenness within us. We fight physical brokenness with all the time and money we have—more than any other element of our wholeness. We may have stopped looking for the mysterious fountain of youth, but we will still buy and try any product that will keep us young. We are the modern offspring of Ponce de Leon.

We spend the most money on our physical wellbeing because our diminishing bodies are so apparent. We see them everyday in the mirror. We are therefore less likely to invest in psychological or emotional therapy because such problems are more covert and can be easily hidden and ignored. And we are even less likely to spend money on spiritual and moral remedies. The rule seems to be as follows: The less tangible the brokenness, the less important the remedy. Thus, physical brokenness seems to always get top billing.

A few years ago, a friend of mine was dying of pancreatic cancer. After my last visit with him I wrote the following in my journal:

> The tumors are legion, and he has only weeks to live. Terry and his wife, Deedee, are strong believers in a loving, faithful God. I am praying for Terry's healing, but he seems to be quickly slipping from our grip.
>
> It is bittersweet to visit with this man who seems to be quite whole in every way but physically. He is a wonderful husband, father, athlete, coach, and friend. In fact, though most people are physically healthier than Terry, they are actually much more broken emotionally, spiritually, or relationally. In so many ways he is whole. Yet he is dying. Wholeness is such an illusive concept to understand. As I drove away from Terry's house I pondered once again, what is wholeness?

Physical wholeness is a huge part of our personal identity and should never be neglected. Jesus spent much of his time healing the sick. Nevertheless, we cannot escape our own mortality. Ultimately our longing for wholeness is much deeper than physical wellbeing. In fact, almost everyone knows someone who is severely handicapped but lives a more fulfilled life than many who are physically healthy. When we interact with such people, we are reminded that a broken inner world is just as in need of remedy as a broken body.

We are ... **Interpersonally (Socially) Broken.** As a young college student and a brand new follower of Jesus, I thought I had almost achieved perfection. My party days were over, and now my life was filled with studies, classes, exercise, eating and sleeping. I had very little room for anything else or anyone else. In a world with just myself, I experienced no anger, greed or lust. In this utopian vacuum I assumed I was almost perfect. Then I met my future wife.

Jan had an amazing impact on me. I wanted to impress her with my experience, knowledge and ability. Aside from vanity and pride, I began to notice lust, anger and impatience rearing their ugly heads. Something was dreadfully wrong. In my naivete I wondered whether she was good for me. This woman, after all, was making me sinful.

Jan and I enjoyed playing our guitars and sharing songs that each other had written. But I clearly remember the first time we tried to write a song together. We thought it would be a fun date. The composition itself was not bad, but the experience was a disaster.

Such experiences point to the conclusion that it's easy to live a "perfect" life without others interacting with us. It is when someone we love doesn't agree with us that problems occur. And these problems are most definitely a brokenness that needs fixing.

Interpersonal relationships aren't all roses. Two people interact with different thoughts, wants, opinions, friends, possessions, dreams and routines. In the brackish water where two different people merge, there is bound to be tension. But this tension is good. If we let it, interpersonal tension sharpens character and alerts us to decisions and changes that need to be made in order to become more whole. Unfortunately, interpersonal tension tends to inflict more brokenness.

We are porcupines, longing to snuggle but finding it hard not to repel each other. We are well aware of the statistics that remind us our marriage has a 50/50 chance of survival. It is understandable why many couples refuse to get married.

The Beatles' melodious observation was not revolutionary, "All You Need is Love." In the naïve 1960's, love, peace and unity seemed so easy and so attainable, but by the 1970's, our naivete was exposed and our innocence lost. To sing about love and to actively love were two very different things. Even the Fab Four broke up.

We are ... **Intrapersonally (Mentally & Emotionally) Broken.** We've always heard that sticks and stones may break our bones but words will never hurt us. We've been misguided. The truth is that we can recover from broken bones but emotional and psychological brokenness can stick with us for a lifetime.

As a seven-year-old, growing up in a neighborhood of rough and tumble boys, I experienced this firsthand. One afternoon we were having chicken fights. When I was finally pushed to the ground, Steve, on whose shoulders I had been riding, timbered on top of me. I put my foot up to bear his weight from crushing me and it snapped the bone in my foot. Unfortunately, my broken bone was not the most painful part.

When I cried out in pain and began sobbing, my friends only laughed. Then not knowing my foot was broken, I struggled to get up, only to have my foot collapse under my weight. My friends laughed harder. Unable to walk and feeling betrayed, I did the only thing a seven-year-old could do; I started crawling home. Seeing me on my hands and knees incited the others to hysterics and mocking. Slowly down the sidewalk I crawled with the painful sounds of my friends behind me. Help did not come until a neighborhood mom noticed me from her kitchen window and ran out to carry me home.

Tragically, every child has a similar awakening to such pain—all too often it leads to brokenness. To survive, most children learn the way of the pack: tease, mock, be cynical and poke fun at everyone else. This keeps the spotlight off us and protects our vulnerable hearts. I learned at that early age of seven that people, even friends, are not always safe, and being the focus of attention with hurtful people is never wise.

Emotional wounds like these stick like glue. Heartbreak is immensely deeper and more lasting than physical pain. The anguish of the loss of a loved one or of personal rejection is suffocating and can last for months or even years. Out of interpersonal brokenness comes intrapersonal brokenness. It is real and it is an important part of our identity.

Intrapersonal brokenness lies latent in all of us. "Intra" refers to the personal issues that exist inside of us, conscious and unconscious, psychological and spiritual, emotional and rational. It is our inner-psychic world. It is "me" and the experience of me. It includes all the inner strata of me that I am both aware of and unaware of: my perceptions, imagination, desires, reasoning and emotions. It includes the parts of the inner me that are unresolved, unforgiven, unhealed and unconsciously disintegrated from the rest of me. Intrapersonal brokenness is a term to describe how out of sync we can become with ourselves.

There is a high price for leaving intrapersonal brokenness untreated. The National Mental Health Association estimates that untreated and mistreated mental illness costs the United States $150 billion in lost productivity each year, and U.S. businesses foot $44 billion of this bill. Workplace stress causes about one million employees to miss work each day. Three out of four employees who seek care for workplace issues or mental health problems see substantial improvement in work performance after treatment. According to the RAND Corporation, depression results in more "bed" days than many other medical ailments, including ulcers, diabetes, high blood pressure and arthritis.[1] Intrapersonal brokenness is nothing to be ignored.

We are ... **Spiritually Broken.** Beneath all the layers of our intrapersonal selves lies the will or the heart. There are various strata of the self: our perception, reasoning, feelings, memories and imaginations. But these parts all seem to be in cahoots with the ringleader of the self—the heart. The heart is the queen bee. If our heart wants something, be it good or bad, our imagination, feelings and reasoning all chime in like a team of lawyers to defend and strengthen the cause. The collective parts of the self rise and fall together around the heart's whims and desires.

What the Greeks referred to as the will and the Hebrews often portrayed as the heart, is a way of describing what we all know to be the core, or essential part, of our being. This spiritual part of us expresses itself through what we choose and the intensity with which we want. We make ourselves distinct and known to others through our heart's choices, preferences and opinions.

There are two clear aspects to every heart: direction and intensity. My heart expresses the directionality of my being. My heart dictates what I choose in both small and big ways. Although it is influenced by input from my senses, my reasoning, my memory and social influence, ultimately the heart decides what I will do, think, say and pursue. It is the weathervane of my being that points to what I truly want most. But is this weathervane always pointing me in the right direction?

Our desire for things is not only at times wrong; it is often far too weak. In *The Weight of Glory*, C. S. Lewis poses that often our behavior is not merely morally wrong but weak. "We are half-hearted creatures," Lewis says, "fooling about with drink and sex and ambition when infinite joy is offered us, like an ignorant child who wants to go on making mud pies in a slum because he cannot imagine what is meant by the offer of a holiday at the sea. We are far too easily pleased."[2]

The heart, with its directionality and intensity, allows me to almost be a god, free to create based on a series of preferences that we have imagined in our mind. The future of life lies in the hands of the human heart. The problem of course is that with the same heart that I give away my time and money, I also will myself to take up the gun and grab the money. I am not a programmed robot nor am I a victim of my environment; I am me, a heart expressed outwardly through opinion, decision and action.

The heart is an amazing tool for good, but there is also something dreadfully broken within it. The heart is broken in its directionality, intensity and its inability to be satisfied.

What I want is sometimes sabotaged by something else I also want. I tell myself, "I should go to church, get some rest, eat right and exercise." In fact, a part of me wants to, but there is something

else in my will, a glitch, a virus, a mutation that often fights the decisions I have previously decided.

It is not simply the directionality of our hearts that is broken—
the intensity is broken as well. Sometimes, I don't want to do the
overridingly good things I know I should, and instead, I intensely
crave the things I know are bad for me to do. The throttle doesn't
seem to give enough gas to the good choices I make, and yet, it gives
plenty of fuel for the bad choices.

Furthermore, there is something in the heart that seems to never
be satisfied. I am content one week and then discontent the next. I
am continually looking for someone or something to refill my heart.
There seems to be an incessant discontent that provokes the heart to
make some very poor choices or to gorge itself with too much of one
thing. There is a hole in my heart and yours that no entertainment,
possession, status or relationship seems to satisfy. Still, my heart won't
stop trying. It behaves as if the final fulfillment is just around the corner time and time again.

* * *

We are broken in many ways, especially at the core of our being.
Regardless of one's theological or spiritual beliefs, an honest anthro-
pological observation of human beings throughout history proves
that we are a spiritually and morally based people. It's not simply that
humans enjoy rituals and stories of the supernatural, but more so that
we actually sense in the core of our beings that we are supposed to
have some sort of connection with the divine. We also seem to corporately agree that how we treat others is the most important moral
issue. It is no coincidence that the two "greatest commands" of which
Jesus spoke hit on these two universal leanings: *Love God with everything you are and love your neighbor as yourself.*

While some will not admit it, we are incapable of escaping either
command. We are obsessed with finding meaning in life, and that
obsession inevitably produces decisions about God's identity and how
other human beings should be treated. This is spirituality, and religious or not, we are all spiritual beings. Even the atheist makes a spir-

itual decision about God and others.

Our souls seem to be imprinted with a faint memory of perfect love, human dignity and paradise itself. This imprint has for centuries been expressed in stories, myths and metaphors. James Loder of Princeton compared our spiritual yearning to that of a child's longing for its mother. He called it the longing for the Face that will never go away.[3]

I am sad sometimes to stroll through the San Diego Zoo and see the animals pacing in their cages. We know their enclosure is not the environment they were designed to inhabit. Although I am thrilled for the opportunity to see African lions and Alaskan brown bears up close, everything about the experience feels wrong. Even after generations of animals born in captivity, these beautiful creatures still look homesick. They, like us, were meant for something more. And so they pace about, as we do, like creatures plagued with perpetual craving. Spiritual creatures with spiritual cravings they can't satisfy in and of themselves.

MUTINY ALL AROUND

This bio-psycho-socio-spiritual brokenness is within us, as well as around us. And for this reason, the simple correlation that good things happen to good people doesn't work. No doubt there is a moderate positive correlation but there are shocking times where bad things happen to good people. Waves of brokenness in our bodies, in nature, in our psyche, in society and in our hearts continue pounding the shores of our being. Sometimes we are the cause, others times we feel the victim. But we mustn't get stuck in this question of theodicy. We leave that to the philosophers to discuss for another millennia. And we must never move in the direction of victim because we will get stuck there too. Our freedom from brokenness must lie in understanding our own hearts.

We are good sailors with a bit of pirate in us. We have committed mutiny over and over again against the good, the true and the beautiful. We are mutated on the surface and at the core of our being, thus disallowing us to fix ourselves.

This is why Jesus said, "I came for those who are sick." He was not inferring that some were well and some were sick and it was only those broken ones for whom he came. His words were directed at the religious leaders of his day who were in denial of their own brokenness. He knew they too were sick too, but they did not and thus failed to see their need for his touch. Perhaps it is a similar story today. The self-sufficient, the healthy, the religiously faithful, the wealthy—these are the ones who tend to think they are not sick, or at least only mildly broken. But it is an illusion. We are all sick in many ways. The first step towards wholeness is this admission.

ADMITTING AND ASCERTAINING OUR BROKENNESS

It is reported that G. K. Chesterton once responded to the question: "What is wrong with the world?" with the vulnerable retort, "I am." His refreshing response is highly unusual. We are far too familiar with our tendency to point the finger at someone else or not at all.

Although we are very comfortable reporting in the daily news the wrongs in the world, we are very uncomfortable talking about what is personally wrong with us. Our defenses and blind spots often keep us from knowing and admitting the underbelly of ourselves.

The church has not been as helpful on this account as she might think. She is quick to remind the world that we are "sinners." Any glance at most church doctrinal statements on the nature of man will read with a resounding "Sinners!" and leave little explanation of what this actually means. We love to elevate certain sins such as adultery, murder and drug abuse but downplay others such as envy, greed, selfishness and gossip. Religion hasn't changed much since the time of Jesus. Religion loves to pick and choose our definition of brokenness.

Not surprisingly, we are far more broken than we care to admit. The denial Freud discerned on the psychological level falls short of our ultimate denial of evil. We hide our faults and weakness to each other and we regularly deny that we are in need of any divine help. Our denial is individual as well as corporate. We don't want to admit we are Humpty Dumpty—fallen, cracked and broken. For millennia, all the king's horses and all the king's men haven't been able to put us together again. Ray Anderson, in *On Being Human*, asserts, "There is no health in us! This is the refrain whenever and wherever honest people take stock of themselves and of their own generation."[4]

So, how broken are we? Our search for wholeness betrays our facade of "togetherness." There is a mutation in our human core that causes an inevitable alienation. This is true of us physically, emotionally, spiritually, interpersonally and intrapersonally. There is something deeply contradictory and tragic about the human condition. The answer to the question above is simply this: We are very broken. Yet, the hope of the world is that wholeness is near.

And the world is right. It is.

chapter four

Broken Masterpieces:
What Does a Whole Person Look Like?

*We have all read in scientific books, and, indeed, in all romances,
the story of the man who has forgotten his name. This man walks
about the streets and can see and appreciate everything; only he
cannot remember who he is. Well, every man has forgotten who he
is. ... We are all under the same mental calamity; we have all forgotten our names. We have all forgotten what we really are.*

— G.K. Chesterton

We were young undergrad students, conscientiously studying in Clark Hall for our midterm in Statistics, when Jan,
my future wife, looked up from her book and stared
across the room. She wore a severe longing on her face. Assuming
that she was rehearsing some thorny statistical equation, I let her be.
But when she lingered in her trance, my inquiry broke the spell. To
my surprise, still staring, she answered in monotone, "I'm longing for
my mom's lemon meringue pie." As I burst out laughing, she turned
to me and smiled. "She makes it very tart, you know, with a very thin,
wafer-crust. I'll have her make us one next time we're home."

The gift of longing is a remarkable human capacity. Nostalgia is
the term we use to describe this sentimental yearning for the familiar.
We humans have the uncanny ability to conjure up past flavors, aro-
mas, faces and places, and make them come alive in the here and now.

The power of nostalgia is so strong it has carried prisoners through untold years of isolation, sailors through the doldrums of the lonely seas, and battle-weary soldiers through the horrors of war. This sort of longing is a wonderful gift indeed. But what of our inexplicable longings that are even deeper than nostalgia? Dreams for things we have never experienced with our senses.

We humans carry an unquenchable longing for transcendent ideals and utopian Neverlands that we have never known. We yearn for things beyond our experience: to be divinely loved, to experience infinite happiness, to find true meaning and value as a person, to discover the peace and beauty of paradise and to live forever. Our poetry and spiritual prose throughout history speak often of these utopian ideals. They seem to indicate that we are originally from a different, much more whole world. Though we have never known a perfect world, we all seem to be trying to get there. Why is that?

How is it that we long for something we have never known and somewhere we have never been? C. S. Lewis argued, "If I find in myself a desire which no experience in this world can satisfy, the most probable explanation is that I was made for another world" since "creatures are not born with desires unless satisfaction for those desires exists…" Therefore, he concludes, followers of Christ must not downplay but keep alive "the desire for their true country, while not despising the earthly blessings that provide a foretaste of it."[1]

WHEN WE WERE PERFECT MASTERPIECES

Lewis experienced and wrote much about this longing for wholeness. He liked to call it a longing for joy, and it was this desire for joy—being wholly who we are created to be—that eventually led him from atheism to faith. His second fantasy book about Narnia, *Prince Caspian*, captures this yearning, as many of his writings do. He describes a young prince growing up with a yearning for a world he has never seen. Stuffy adults tell him the world he desires does not exist. Still, the stories he has heard from his nanny feed this longing all the more—stories of talking badgers, valiant Centaurs, dryads and the great Lion from beyond the sea, Aslan. The adventure eventually leads him to discover an unseen world has always existed and it is home to him. He eventually becomes the rightful king of Narnia, fulfilling the longing stirring inside him all his years. It is a story about a broken person becoming whole.

Lewis firmly believed this longing for a whole world—for Narnia—resides in all of us. His story of Prince Caspian was written as a reminder of something that had been lost. He felt the modernist's world had neutered the longing, blurring our perception of God and the spiritual. He also felt Christianity itself had given up the power of pixie dust found in our hearts' pursuit of wholeness, in order to appear legitimate to the world of modernity, a world built on dry reason and empiricism alone.

Consequently, many who search today for the source of this universal desire, turn to Eastern religion to escape the cold steel apologist's approach to faith. Others come to Christian faith, but remain icy in their approach to life, biding their time, waiting for a wholeness that will come eventually. Lewis instead believed we continue to long for another world by constantly trying "to get in."[2] He thus used the power of fairytales to sneak past the gatekeepers of modernists' hearts.

It was this inexplicable longing that also began my transformation, or as I call it, my surrender. For me, the moments of acute longing seemed to whisper to my soul, "You were made for more." It was usually when I was alone that I heard it and this convinced me even more. I believed there had to be a bigger reason to live. I was healthy, exercising, eating healthy foods and even meditating. But the longing persisted, and I insisted the purpose of life couldn't be to simply get a job, get married, have babies, collect things and then die. I once desperately cried out to heaven, "All I ever wanted to be is the man you created me to be." I just didn't know who that was or how that was accomplished.

It was only later that I found my answer in the ancient writing of *Genesis*. The book's inspired author felt what I felt and described an answer that rang true in my soul. There I found that my longing was to become a person who was matched with God's blueprint for me as a human being. I realized then that I had lived much of my life in a subhuman way—being everything except who I was created to be. I wondered if my longing was really a common yearning, part of a sub-conscious, collective memory that everyone carries from an ancient, faultless beginning that we call paradise. I read about and longed for the world of Eden where the majesty of creation connected with my heart. My longing felt like homesickness for a world I'd never known. I've now come to learn that's precisely what it was and still is for us all.

Any definition of a whole, healed or saved person must reckon with this longing for how things should be. All of us long for things to be whole, beautiful and as they were meant to be. The problem is that we often do the easy thing; we dismiss this longing as childish, as neurotic or a biological longing for the womb. In truth, we long for God, the things of God and the revealing of our definition in Him. It is in the primordial creation story that we find a definition of a whole human being that resonates deeply with our souls but doesn't split us from our bodies.

In the creation story we find a bio-psycho-socio-spiritual model of human wholeness that surpasses all other definitions. This ancient passage clearly declares that our substance and purpose is found in the image of God—the Imago Dei. This is the stark difference. *Genesis* says that our identity is not found in ourselves but in another. The whole person I long to be is found in God's identity.

THE IMAGE OF GOD

> *And the end of all our exploring*
> *Will be to arrive where we started*
> *And know the place for the first time.*
> —T.S. Elliot, *Little Gilding*

In a trite world where Darwin and Christian bumper fish battle for superiority, it is easy for us to miss the ultimate intent of the creation story. In this elegant Hebrew narrative God unveils his intent in creating humankind. In the stratosphere of this revelation, we learn not only of our exalted identity as humans but also of our global, down-to-earth mandate. It is in this passage where we discover that true wholeness is not of this world but in fact "an alien wholeness."[3]

Without question the rhythm and momentum of the creation narrative reaches its zenith in verses 26-28 of Genesis 1:

> Then God said, "Let us make man in our image, in our likeness, and let them rule over the fish of the sea and the birds of the air, over the livestock, over all the earth, and over all the creatures that move along the ground." So God created man in his own image, in the image of God he created him; male and female he created them. God blessed them and said to them, "Be fruitful and increase in number; fill the earth and subdue it. Rule over the fish of the sea and the birds of the air and over every living creature that moves on the ground."

In these verses we hear God speak dramatically in his plural of majesty—*Let us*. Such deliberation in the regal, plurality of God allows the reader to instantly know something major is about to happen. This last act of creation will be his masterpiece.

The unfaltering, poetic drumbeat of the previous days of creation is broken here. Each day has been a simple command, *and God said, "Let there be..."* But this unique creative act draws God into a holy huddle where he thinks out loud in front of us. He doesn't just speak humankind into existence. The blueprint and intention is agreed upon verbally in advance, and then he follows through by creating the pinnacle of creation—man and woman.

We instantly know why this creative act is the zenith. Three phrases used in the blueprint description tip us off: *our image, our likeness* and *rule over*. Nowhere else in the preceding account of creation has there been any statement of this magnitude. In the first two words, *image* and *likeness*, we discover the clue for fulfilling our identity. God's intent is for us is to look like God in someway, finding our identity in his face, his character, his nature. In the last phrase, *rule over*, we discover our mandate or purpose on earth. We are to represent God to the rest of creation. Therefore, our identity and purpose is spelled out both vertically and horizontally. We are to be creatures, who in some way, look like God and reflect his glory to creation. With one hand we touch God's face and with the other we reach out to the world.

The writer of this account is so stunned at this possibility that he repeats himself to be sure that we have comprehended what he has just said: *So God created man in his own image, in the image of God he created him (27).* The writer seems dumfounded at his own writing. Could it be that God would share of himself in such a dynamic and personal way?

The Hebrew term for *image* is the same term used for *idol* or *icon.* Although Israel was forbidden to have any false gods or idols, the passage indicates that humans were designed to be the single, living icon representing God. We are idols of God not to be worshipped, but to represent God to others. We are living statues of God's likeness. Like coins stamped with the image of a Caesar, creation stamped the image of God on man and woman.

But the questions remain: If we are made in his image, what does God look like? Is looking like God what it means to be whole? Certainly his "image" cannot refer to characteristics such as omniscience, omnipresence or omnipotence. It must therefore be referring to something in God's nature that we share with him. It is, as you will see, the face of wholeness.

GOD-LIKE DESIRES

We as humans have an intuitive sense for goodness, love and truth. No one needs to tell us when something is good or bad. We know it, even as a small child. In a similar way, we know when love is happening without someone telling us. Although we are selfish and often fail to love unconditionally, we have no problem recognizing love or being touched by acts of compassion. We also have an innate sense of truth. Although truth has been made "relative" in recent generations, all humans live with a sense of rightness and justice. When something is not right, we express our displeasure. When justice is not being served, we rally with signs and chants.

While we are clearly not always acting in goodness, love and truth, we retain the instinct for them no matter what. We can stifle, ignore or blur these instincts, but they eventually come out in one manifestation or another. Their stickiness indicates that the blueprint for wholeness has been implanted upon us.

We are in many ways objectively and permanently made in God's image. But what is obvious, and perhaps most important, is that we share in God's desire for goodness, love and truth. This is incredibly significant where our pursuit of wholeness is concerned. When we embody our God-like desires, we are effectively acting out of wholeness. To show goodness ... to love unconditionally ... to promote truth and justice is to be whole. The more we embody these characteristics, the more whole we become with each action.

While we are certainly no mirror image of God in these three arenas, we are nonetheless extremely powerful creatures with an ability, through one act of goodness, love or truth, to change the life of another. For this reason alone, we ought to honor each other and protect each other's dignity.

It is sad, and perhaps even inconsiderate, that many churches have their first statement about the nature of man remind us that we are sinners. Although this is certainly true, it is not God's first statement of us. Furthermore, sin has no meaning without the contrast of God's divine intent for us. If we, the Christian church, are to speak of human beings, our first statement should attempt to be as lofty as God's: wholeness in his image.

Perhaps this is why I have always appreciated the eastern greeting, with the folding of the hands before my face. I know of its pantheistic origins, recognizing the deity in the other person, but I have instead allowed it to mean recognizing the image of God in another. In fact, the Christians of Nepal still practice this beautiful gesture substituting the Hindu greeting, *Namaste* for *Jai Masahi*, which means "Victory to the Messiah!"

I have walked for miles at the base of the Himalayas without passing a soul. Then out of the blue appears a person, not simply an animal, but a human soul made in the image of God. As they approach I raise my hands to my face and bow. She is made in the image of God and something about her is an indication of what a whole person looks like—what victory looks like. She is a broken masterpiece, yes, but a broken masterpiece still looks, at certain angles, quite like a masterpiece.

C. S. Lewis captures this truth better than anyone:

> It is a serious thing to live in a society of possible gods and goddesses, to remember that the dullest and most uninteresting person you talk to may one day be a creature which, if you saw it now, you would be strongly tempted to worship... It is in the light of these overwhelming possibilities, it is with the awe and the circumspection proper to them, that we should conduct all our dealings with one another, all friendships, all loves, all play, all politics. There are no 'ordinary' people. You have never talked to a mere mortal.[4]

The point here is simple but profound: We are made in the image of God by nature. Though we fail to reflect God's image wholly, we are nevertheless hardwired to be like God, evidenced by our inherent desires and the carrying out of those desires. But it is through the nurture of our relationship with him that we ultimately reflect his glory—the glory that was displayed in Jesus on earth.

GOD'S IMAGE IN RELATIONSHIPS

Our sharing of the image of God is not only hard-wired into our nature; it is existentially affected by the quality of our relationship with God—by nurture. We are in nature and nurture made in the image of God.

If we return to the Genesis text, the immediate context defines the image as having to do with love and relationship. The plurality in the language is the key: *let us ... our image ... our likeness*. God-in-community created us to be like him. The relationship of *male* and *female* also makes it clear that we too are designed in this way—to be in community. God himself lives in eternal love and community within himself (the Trinity) and we are designed for the same purpose—to live in community with each other and with him.

By stating in the passage that the image is *male and female* (Genesis 1:27), the writer is both hinting at the deeper meaning of *image*, and making a clarification. In clarifying, the writer is ensuring that the reader understands that both genders are made in God's image. The clarification is helpful in a male dominated world to ensure that women are given the same dignity as men. The clarification states that all people, regardless of gender, are made in the image of God. But he is even saying more than that.

The writer is also implying that *image* involves relationship. Since God exists in his *us*-ness (*let us... our*), as bearers of his image, we too are whole when we exist within a community. And not just any community, but the community in which God lives—in true love.

Though we are hard-wired for community, it is clear we don't have the power within ourselves for perfect community. It is in the vertical relationship, the nurturing of our relationship with God, that we discover this power to commune like him. Lewis sums it up this way:

> God designed the human machine to run on Himself. He Himself is the fuel our spirits were designed to burn, or the food our spirits were designed to feed on. There is no other. That is why it is just not good asking God to make us happy in our own way without bothering about religion. God cannot give us a happiness and peace apart from Himself, because it is not there. There is no such thing.[5]

It is important for us to remember that we are not spiritual containers of God. We are only vessels designed to give his attributes away to each other and to creation. In this way, we truly love God by loving others (see John 15:12; 1 John 3:11). In this way, loving others, we are acting out of wholeness.

For certain, we fall short of perfect consistency in this arena, but this does not mean we cannot continue to improve as our relationship with God increases in intimacy.

And the truth is that we all have acquaintances but only a few dozen qualify as friends. Even friendship usually surrounds one or two commonalities. Only one to three may be a true friend with whom I share everything in life. In that friendship there is perfect respect, trust, openness, as well as no fear of betrayal, judgment or shame. In relationships like these, we share our pearls and they are polished and appreciated by the other, not trampled in the mud. The communication is in the moment, unguarded, and flowing freely because we understand so much of each other. We may move freely between laughter to tears without a thought of ourselves.

The result of such whole relationships is not unlike Moses' experience in the desert. As he spent time with God, the glory of God would cause Moses' face to shine. The Apostle Paul sums this increasing wholeness in this way: And we, who with unveiled faces all reflect the Lord's glory, are being transformed into his likeness with ever-increasing glory, which comes from the Lord, who is the Spirit (2 Corinthians 3:18).

Ultimately, without intimacy with God and others, I cannot become who I am made to be—I cannot become whole. This wholeness is defined by ever-increasing vertical and horizontal relationships. Without a loving and faithful relationship with God I am without an identity—I have no target of wholeness. Without others to love in community, I am without a purpose and I am not whole.

THE IMPLICATIONS OF THE IMAGO DEI

The point is clear—our identity, our face, is found in the face of God, in both nature and nurture. Our mandate is to shine that face to creation. We are not the Face, but are made to reflect the Face. The good news of this definition of a whole human is that we are God's viceroys on earth. King man, and queen woman; we speak and act for God. *What is man that you are mindful of Him?... You have made him a little lower than the Elohim* (the plural form of the word used for God or the angels) (Psalm 8:4-5).

But, in the intoxication of this amazing revelation, there is also some bad news. The bad news for autonomous humans is that we were made to reflect Another's face, not our own. Without God, we have no identity, no wholeness. It is God's design and there is no other. We can argue or disagree with the law of gravity but it is engineered into creation. In the same way, we can argue about who we are and how we are to become whole, but at the end of the day, we are made to reflect God's nature and that's how we become whole.

If we autonomously break from God's intent, our nature is still dependent on another. We are hard-wired to look for someone or something else to define us. It is impossible in our design to live autonomously without an image to model. If it is not God, we will search and long for something else to define us. If it is not God, we may find our identity in our accomplishments, our possessions, our heritage or in our talent. But we will never be wholly who we are made to be.

The Cry of a Broken-Hearted Father

Like the first couple, one temptation is always before us: to find our independent wholeness, our full humanity, in something other than Creator God. It's the temptation to turn from being willing to being willful.[6] At its core, this act is the substitution of our dependent relationship with God to a mystical control of our own universe. It's when king man and queen woman no longer represent God, but instead, themselves. The stench of pride is always present as we move from an innocent, loving relationship with God to arrogant autonomy, which according to God's design is inhuman.

Yet, in one act, one choice, one freewill decision, the first couple betrayed not only God, but themselves as well. We are tempted daily in much the same way. Scripture tells us the first couple was already "like God" but they wanted more. They were already intelligent, creative, loving and spiritual, but they wanted more. They were already king man and queen woman, but they wanted more. They wanted everything of the nature of God without being dependent upon him. And in one fell swoop they lost everything—and so did we.

"Surely die," was the warning. And die they did. But not, perhaps as they expected. There was no immediate physical death. That came later. Nevertheless, death in the greatest sense of the word now begins to cover Eden like a fog, and earth itself begins to silently heave over the loss of its appointed ambassadors. They (and we) are separated from the face of God and subsequently, any creation that sees God's face through the ambassadors' image is separated as well. All of creation is now longing.

Not only are there the immediate consequences of shame and broken fellowship with God and each other, but also death exponentially grows verse by verse and chapter to chapter. Now the brothers, Cain and Abel, will do the unthinkable, commit a jealous murder for religious reasons (Genesis 4). Now godly people will compromise their values by marrying ungodly spouses and raising their children in ungodly ways spreading wickedness and ruthlessness (Genesis 6). God himself, in an anthropomorphic sigh of emotional pain, even regrets his creation of humankind (Genesis 6:6). Finally, the brokenness becomes international and racial, represented by the fall of the tower of Babel (Genesis 11). Step by step, generation after generation, the consequences of the original attempt at autonomous wholeness are felt throughout the world.

MIRROR, MIRROR ON THE WALL...

That is the painful story of the loss of wholeness. The perfect spiritual ecosystem of Eden instantly crumbled and left an eternal impact on humankind. The trust and love that kept it together is now gone. Without the face of God, Adam and Eve now "know" something they had never known—shame. Rather than becoming the gods they'd hoped they would—alas, his face was already ours—they have only the mirrored knowledge of their nakedness, their incompleteness. They are now only aware of who they are not. Inadequacy, insecurity, humiliation, shame and embarrassment are suddenly theirs and ours. These embody knowledge, indeed, but not the knowledge they had hoped for. We are their descendants: people made to be whole, aware only of our un-wholeness—and thus ever-seeking a cure to be whole once again.

Like potato heads without a face, we modern Adams and Eves

must now dig through the box of life to find our identity and purpose. We try on this and that but it never quite fits. It is not who we are. We are unfulfilled. We are someone more important, more significant, but we can't remember why. Now we live with a sense, not of who we are, but of who we aren't. We are always left with the longing for something more, the hollow longing we can all recognize.

We all know the story of the emperor's new clothes, where some swindler tailors came to town promising to make him the finest and most beautiful clothes in the kingdom. They make his new clothes literally out of "whole cloth," which is invisible to the eye. Only they tell the king and other courtiers that only the wise and noble can see the material. Through peer pressure everyone in the court pretends to see the clothes. Finally, the day comes when the king parades his new cloths for the entire kingdom to see. It takes a child to break the spell by shouting "the king has no clothes on." In that instant the king heard what he feared all along: his clothed identity was a sham. We are all the king.

We attempt to find our identity in something outside ourselves because that is our nature. Without a divine face to behold and find our identity, we turn to other things. Just as the ancients turned to other gods and deities made in their own image, we turn to other things as well. We look to find our identity in possessions, positions and important relationships. Our beauty, wit and accomplishments weigh much heavier on the social scales of significance and so we behave in ways that say, "This is why you should regard me as important." Listen to yourself the next time you are at a party where you don't know anyone. You will do and say things to let the others know, "I really am important, you just don't know me yet." But eventually someone sees through it all.

If our identity by design was to reflect God and our mandate was to serve creation with his nature, it stands to reason that any mutiny against that design would lead to disaster. The warning from God was that the couple would surely die. But the death was far more than physical. We lost our identity. A bird can't cease to be a bird and an antelope can't cease to be an antelope, but our ancestors chose to attempt to be inhuman. Now we all wander the earth living subhuman lives.

The *Genesis* story not only tells us of the birth of sin, refusing to want and find our glory in God; it also tells the beginning of every vice imaginable. It is one thing to be guilty of a particular sin; it is another to be shame-based, not confident in one's identity. The end result becomes insecurity, timidity, unconfidence, anxiety and fear. Out of these come all the interpersonal sins of rage, anger and passive aggressive behaviors attempting to control each other. Out of these come acts of sin, wounding and harming others made in the image. It is individual and international. All which perpetuate the brokenness.

Once this is understood the tragedy of the fall becomes apparent. It is clear that the temptation of Adam and Eve was to step out from under the nature of perfect wholeness. The vain and wicked queen of *Snow White and the Seven Dwarves* continually retraced her steps to her tower to insecurely ask the mirror, "Mirror, mirror on the wall, who is the fairest of them all?" Day by day the magical mirror assured her she was the fairest in the kingdom, until one fateful day she heard the words she dreaded, that someone else had replaced her. "Queen, you are full fair, 'tis true, but Snow White is fairer than you."

The wicked queen is not that different from all of us. We run to something, someone, someplace, some activity, some attachment to find our identity. But it is tentative and temporary. One day something happens and my identity and worth are gone.

Sadly, when I walk down the streets of San Diego, I don't stop and stare at a person because they look so much like God. I don't say, "Boy, he looks like God!" Yet, that was God's intent. We all have fallen and the image of God in us is smeared, often beyond recognition. Now I walk the streets as a hollow man with the rest of the hollow humanity.

It is typical of us to autonomously pick our cures. When it comes to being whole, as with every other area of our lives, we prefer to be the authors of our own destiny. And out of this attitude, we will decide if we need a therapist, a trainer, some yoga, a physician or a plastic surgeon. I will be whole my own way and I will determine when I am whole. But without consulting the Wholly Image, our pursuit of wholeness is bound to fail; if not immediately, eventually. If we are to find ourselves whole, we must find the Wholly One.

JESUS: THE WHOLLY IMAGE OF GOD

From the moment a newborn's searching eyes behold this complicated world, a game begins. It is an internal game of hide-and-seek revolving around the self. The infant's primary mission is to find love and meaning in life. There is a built-in belief in every child that love and meaning truly exist and that the child will find itself there. Too young to comprehend this longing, the child looks for meaning and love in the simple faces around it. Particularly in the face of the mom and dad, the child searches for its own value and meaning. But ultimately, the child is seeking, in James Loder's words, "the Face that will never go away."[7] It is this Face who knows the meaning of the child's existence. It is this face for which we all search.

One day the Face we longed for came—the Face that showed us our wholly identity. *"That which was from the beginning, which we have heard, which we have seen with our eyes, which we have looked at and our hands have touched—this we proclaim concerning the Word of life."* (1 John 1:1) *"We have seen his glory, the glory of the One and Only, who came from the Father, full of grace and truth"* (John 1:14). *"He is the image of the invisible God, the firstborn over all creation"* (Colossians 1:15). What the Book of Revelation promises in the end, *"[We] shall see his face…"* (Revelation 22:4) happened in advance. What we lost in the first garden was offered to us again in Jesus.

For this reason, the New Testament refers to Jesus as the second Adam, once again a whole human reflecting the glory of God. Jesus is called *the image of God* (2 Corinthians 4:4). Furthermore, the New Testament promises that those who follow Jesus will be like him (Romans 8:29) and are thus being transformed into the image of God (2 Corinthians 3:18; Romans 12:2). Jesus, in other words, is the objective of full humanity—the human example of wholeness.

John declares, "We have seen his glory, the glory of the One and Only, who came from the Father, full of grace and truth" (John 1:14). Jesus' story and ours is full of unusual hope. In Jesus, we not only find wholeness but we discover ourselves. Yet Jesus' offer is from an upside down world: "Whoever finds his life will *lose* it, and whoever loses his life for *my sake* will find it" (Matthew 10:39). With the whole world pursuing wholeness, it is time we reconsider God's design and his method for making us whole. We are broken masterpieces[8]—designed for wholeness but possessing only a faint and distant memory of what that looks like. Jesus came to remind us.

Even though we lost ourselves in the fall, and brokenness has mutated just about every area of our lives, there is still something of the image of God that shines through in every person. Though we have lost our identity, we have wholly instincts that are deeper still. A mother or father still knows how to love their newborn child; we still have faint stirrings of a whole creation when we see something beautiful in nature. We long to be whole and to behold wholeness. We are broken masterpieces waiting for restoration. And our restorer has come.

PART II:

HOW JESUS DEFINED WHOLENESS

chapter five

The Invasion Has Begun

Enemy-occupied territory—that is what this world is. Christianity is the story of how the rightful king has landed, you might say landed in disguise, and is calling us all to take part in a great campaign of sabotage.

— C.S. Lewis

I can only remember one blind date in my teenage years where a friend set me up and we went on a double date. I had no idea what she would look like or how she would act. But as the day approached my expectations grew. In my mind, I was about to date the most beautiful, fascinating girl in the world—Miss America!

What a disappointment. We had absolutely nothing in common. I'm sure both of us regretted the night. Who we thought we were going out with and who actually showed up that night were two very different people. We never saw each other again.

Jesus, too, is a blind date. Expectations are everything. There must be hundreds of thousands of paintings of Jesus. What is on the canvas is an expectation in the mind of the artist even though no one knows what he looked like during his time on Earth. Most people envision Jesus with long hair because of recorded mystical visions, the imprint on the shroud and confusion between a Nazarite vow and Jesus' hometown of Nazareth. But that image is quite questionable considering most religious men of his day wore their hair short. And for all men it was considered a "shame" to have long hair (1

Corinthians 11:14). If we are wrong about his hair length, what other misconceptions might we have?

Like a blind date, we often come to Jesus with our preconceptions and try to force him into our mold. We can't help it. We see the world through our lenses of experience and core beliefs. We can't escape our subjective biases. Atheists, Hindus, Buddhists, Muslims, Pagans, New Agers and Christians of all stripes do the same. Usually the image of Jesus is positive in some way, but the mold is pre-cast and we pour Jesus and his teachings into what we already believe. Consequently, we often miss the real Jesus—the Wholly Jesus.

JESUS HISTORICALLY EMERGES

Out of the faceless town of Nazareth he emerged. The time had come. His message was bold, unassuming and compelling: "Repent, the kingdom of heaven is near." *Turn from how you are living; God's invading will and desire is coming close to you!*

God's advancing kingdom was his constant theme. Jesus preached this message in the liturgy of the local synagogue, out in the open fields before the pressing masses, amidst controversial debates with the religious teachers, even within the danger zone of the Jerusalem Temple courts. Using illustrative stories from daily village life called parables, he both explained and concealed the meaning of *the kingdom*. When he healed people miraculously, he acted out the heart, or will, of *God's kingdom*. Even at his death his kingdom message was unavoidable. Pilot insisted that the sign above his head should read: *the king of the Jews*. Kingship was his only legal crime.

But what did his listeners hear? Why were his disciples so loyal and yet often so confused? Why were the religious teachers and leaders both intrigued and enraged? Why were the masses together enchanted and ultimately rejecting? And why were the political leaders equally curious and threatened?

There is no doubt the Jews of Jesus' day were expecting *the Messiah*. The land was abuzz with heightened anticipation. The Qumran community (of the Dead Sea Scrolls) alone illustrates this expectation. In fact, some may have even been looking for more than one messiah, a royal messiah and one from the priesthood. Other false messiahs arose and others were yet to come.

The title meant *anointed one* (*Christos* was merely a Greek translation of the Hebrew term *Messiah*). Over and over again the term appeared as the ancient Jewish writers of the Bible penned their prophetic longings onto parchment. The Messiah was the One who was to come, as the prophets had foretold, and restore to Israel the golden years of his ancestor David. He was to be a deliverer who challenged the oppressor and defended the oppressed. He was to announce a time of jubilee for the nation when all the wrongs, debts and injustices of the land would be made right. And although he was the one for whom all Israel had longed for, there was much debate about his kingship. Because of this confusion, Jesus chose a different title for himself—son of man.

This title was enigmatic, humble and bold all at once. To some, the title was simply poetic; to others, the self-designation was a statement of humility and commonality—"I'm a man; I'm one of you." But it was also a bold, heavenly title.

In using the title, son of man, Jesus was claiming, "I am the coming, heavenly Messiah foretold by the Scriptures" (see Daniel 7:13). But the title was enigmatic enough to camouflage Jesus' identity from those who only wanted a messiah who would fulfill their selfish expectations. At the same time, the title openly revealed Jesus with his full, robust agenda to those who sought him as he was—those who sought Wholly Jesus.

EXPECTATIONS ARE EVERYTHING

The interpretation of the prophets' predictions of the messiah took on many different faces. For the political activists like the Zealots, the messiah would deliver Israel from Roman rule, restoring their land to political freedom and he would reign in power from Jerusalem. The Messiah was to do what Judas Maccabeus, their historical hero of the 2nd century BC, did when he led his nation in revolt against the aging Syrian-Greek kingdom of Antiochus Epiphanes. In Jesus' day, some messianic radicals had already arisen and more were to come. For the 1st century BC political activist, Jesus' kingdom message meant freedom from Rome the oppressor and self-rule regained for Israel. They dreamed of once again enjoying the expansive, powerful kingdom of the great King David, a thousand years before. They expected liberation and nothing short of this expectation would do.

King Herod expected, and feared, a political messiah that could rob him of his throne. This insecure ruler of Israel, half Jewish, half Edomian (modern day Jordanian), was a puppet of the Roman Empire. It is clear from the story of Jesus' birth in the gospel of Matthew that King Herod the Great was very threatened by the potential arrival of the messiah and his kingdom. Although Herod's wealth was vast and his rule was firm, any threat, whether real or perceived, was dealt with instantly and severely. Herod's own sons were no exception; history records their bloody murders at Herod's hand. By the time of Jesus' death, one of Herod's sons ruled the nation, but his curiosity and fear of a political messiah were no less than his father's.

For the followers of John the Baptist, the message of the kingdom had a more pietistic bent. Whether John the Baptist was nurtured in the ways of the Qumran community or simply had many things in common, scholars still speculate; but what is clear is that both groups represented a large pietistic population of Israel. They expected the messiah to deal with the hearts of the people and their unrighteous behavior. They were looking for the messiah to bring an inner transformation from sins before God and this was to be measured by how they treated others. The messiah would bring the nation back to God and to his holy Torah.

Perhaps for the masses, the expectations were a mishmash of various ideas. Like voters today of a presidential campaign, their hopes varied. The poor and broken peasant—those who knew best the brokenness of the world—wanted only for God to fix things.

Jesus chose followers from these various streams. He dipped heavily into the group who had followed or had been influenced by John the Baptist. Peter, Andrew, James, John and Nathaniel all came from this group. Matthew was a despised tax collector and therefore a friend to Rome. He was a Jew who made his money (mostly unfairly) off of his fellow kinsmen by collecting taxes for oppressive Rome. Simon, not Peter, was the only Zealot. Zealots were religious/political activists who mixed their faith with activism. They had and were prepared to take up arms against Rome. There were also some wealthier followers, some who were close to the palace, like Joanna whose husband managed Herod's household, and others who were among the religious congress called the Sanhedrin, such as Nicodemus and Joseph of Arimathea (Mark 15:43; John 19:38, 39).

Although it was a man's world in the 1st century, there were various women who boldly followed Jesus; they were not part of the twelve, but they were nonetheless disciples in the broad sense. Mary and Martha, sisters of his friend Lazarus, are good examples (Luke 10:39). Other women such as Joanna, Mary Magdalene and Susanna helped support Jesus and the disciples financially (Luke 8:1-3).

With disciples from varied backgrounds came varied expectations for the messiah. We can see how controversial and confusing Jesus' actions and teachings were to the people of his day. Even John the Baptist, his cousin, was confused and sent his disciples to ask Jesus, *"Are you the one who was to come, or should we expect someone else?"* (Matthew 11:3). Jesus, himself, highlighted the confusion when he asked his own disciples, "Who do people say I am?" (Mark 8:27).

Jesus' message certainly fit the 1st century cultural messianic expectation, but his followers carried preconceived notions as to the nature of the messiah. They assumed the messiah would fit their expectations. These strong expectations emerge in various passages: when James' and John's mother requested that her sons be given seating prominence at Jesus' throne (Matthew 20:20-23); when Peter rebukes Jesus for speaking of the cross (Matthew 16:22); and possibly when Judas betrayed Jesus. Biases driven by personal needs and religious or social expectations can be fierce. These very same cultural expectations and personal biases not only existed in the 1st century; they exist in the 21st century.

SHRINKING JESUS

I hate to go to a barber or hair stylist who cuts everyone's hair alike. They ask you how you want your hair, then they cut it they way they cut everyone else's. All of the customers walk out looking like clones. We are all guilty of applying this cookie-cutter approach to some part of life, especially to the things we know little about. We are famous for our generalizations and stereotypes. We even do this to Jesus, giving him our culturally expected haircut. Just as each of the followers of Jesus had their expectations 2,000 years ago, we, today, also have our own. Our expectations almost always shrink the nature of Jesus to fit within our worldview.

There are four common types of Jesus in the Western world today: 1) the pop-Christian Jesus, 2) the socially concerned Jesus, 3) the contemplative Jesus, and 4) the naturalistic Jesus. There are various other faces of Jesus but they are often subsets of these four. Although these overlap at times, they are very distinctive to the outsider. Though we cannot escape our biases, we must become aware of them, learn to laugh at ourselves, and allow Jesus to shape us rather than the reverse.

Pop-Christian Jesus. The most popular Jesus of America is the pop-Christian Jesus. He lives in the suburbs, votes republican and listens strictly to contemporary Christian music. He drives an SUV to protect his family in case of an accident and uses it to shuttle his children to Christian school. His large car wears a sticker of a fish eating Darwin to help defeat evolution in America.

His stance toward culture is one of protection—Christ against culture.[1] He is against all the changes in culture coming out of Hollywood (media), Boston (education), New York (Wall Street) and Washington (politics). Consequently, he withdraws from much of mainstream life to protect himself and remain holy until heaven.

To protect himself from the world, his home and church are much like a castle. These places are refuges from the temptations of the world. Although, he leaves the castle like a knight for an evangelistic crusade, to watch a soccer or baseball game, or to vote; the rest of the time, he is at church. The primary moral and political issues that concern him surround protecting his children from drugs, abortion, evolution and homosexuality. Salvation for the pop-Christian Jesus is one of escape from sin and this earth. His favorite book series is *Left Behind*. The kingdom of God for this Jesus is primarily upward, saving souls for heaven. People are either in or they're out.

Pop-Christian Jesus is loving and kind, until you deviate from the party line. Then his gavel is swift and heavy. He controls the Christian radio and TV waves, and much of the Christian publishing in America. To the pop-Christian follower, there is no other Jesus.

Socially-concerned Jesus. For this Jesus, the kingdom of God is primarily outward. Although he has been around a long time, primarily among those who are theologically liberal, he is gaining in popularity among the young evangelicals. He has moved to the inner-city to get into the arts and identify with the poor. He, unlike the pop-Christian Jesus, is free to enjoy wine or beer in moderation. He votes moderate-to-liberal, subscribes to *Sojourners* magazine and enjoys poetry, coffee houses and existential philosophy. He is non-judgmental of everyone except rightwing pop-Christians.

In his desire to reach out to the lost in love he is often unclear as to what the Bible says about Scriptural authority, sexual morality and identity, salvation and divine judgment. He would rather have a conversation than debate doctrine. His moral agenda centers on helping the poor and saving the planet. He is against war and thinks its wasteful expense should be used for education, housing and aid. For him, living life to the fullest is everything. He is not concerned about heaven or hell, but rather how he lives in the existential moment. This is the Jesus of post-modernity. His cultural stance is Christ into or transforming culture.[2] He wants to be involved, make friends and influence Hollywood, New York and Washington. To the post-modern believer, this Jesus is the only Jesus.

Contemplative Jesus. For him, the kingdom of God is primarily inward. He lives in liturgical churches, he is close with monks and he loves to meditate. Crosses, candles, bells and incense are all vital symbols to his meditative lifestyle. The evangelical expression of this movement is found in what is called spiritual formation or spiritual theology. He visits monasteries, reads books and attends conferences that encourage internal formation and transformation. He has great interest in the practices of the Eastern Orthodox church, he reads Thomas Merton and he enjoys dialoguing with those with an Eastern

philosophy. This Jesus is sensitive to the planet and others, and he
speaks softly, if at all. His cultural stance is *Christ above culture*.[33]

Naturalistic Jesus. Then there is the Jesus of naturalism. This is
the Jesus Seminar savior. He does not have a large following, but he
is quite powerful on university campuses. This messiah has been sliced
and diced to look an awful-lot like a critical theologian. He wears
bifocals and carries a briefcase with a laptop. He knows many ancient
languages, and on his vacations he participates in an archeological dig.
This Jesus can't and wouldn't dare do any miracles. He is unclear as
to his own identity and mission. Whoever he is he must be different
than the Apostle Paul's manufactured Jesus. This Jesus is a professor
of ethics to help us reapply the Torah for today. He lives in constant
hangover from the Enlightenment. This Jesus is primarily historical.
His cultural stance is *Christ of the first century culture*.[4]

WHICH JESUS IS WHOLLY?

There are certainly other faces for Jesus: the Scottish-
Presbyterian-preacher Jesus, the seeker-friendly hip Jesus, the south-
ern gospel Jesus, the culturally-relevant Jesus, the handclapping-
Charismatic Jesus, the rock-n-roll hippy Jesus, the promise-keeping
Jesus and the health-and-prosperity Jesus. Finally, there is the stand-
back-and-cynically-criticize-everyone-else Jesus. In reality, Jesus of the
Western world has as many faces as there are Christians. Amazingly, he
still always looks like us.

While every face of Jesus is easily criticized, especially by one of
the other manifestations, they each have strengths and weaknesses.
But if we humble ourselves, we must admit honestly that we are
drawn to the passages of Scripture that promote our particular expectation of Jesus. Even when we are in a convicting or challenging portion of Scripture, we emerge with a dismissal of the threat and a con-
firmation of our expectation. Our chosen preachers even help to keep
our Jesus Jell-O mold strong.

Sadly, we have ultimately shrunk the image of Jesus. Our personal wants and cultural worldviews have reduced and minimized Wholly
Jesus and his wholeness message. Rarely, do we make him and his

message bigger; instead, Jesus' message usually conveys just what we want it to. Rarely do we hear the gunshot message that woke the world of the 1st century ... that drove him out of Nazareth, that attracted the followers to leave everything behind and that eventually enraged the religious leaders and nailed him to the cross. Jesus' whole message is sweet and sour, comforting and threatening, heaven and earth, leading to both healing and to persecution. But ultimately, this message was offered to return this world to wholeness—the wholeness we had in the beginning, in the first garden.

If we are to be transformed into his wholly image, we must allow Jesus to be himself. At least the best we can, knowing we never escape our own reducing subjectivity. So what is the simple, unrefined message of Jesus and the invading kingdom?

JESUS' CORE MESSAGE

"The time has come," he said. *"The kingdom of God is near. Repent and believe the good news!"* (Mark 1:15). His message was not totally new. It was the central message of his predecessor, John the Baptist (Matthew 3:2). Before him, it was the prophetic message and hope of the Torah or Old Testament (Daniel 2:44; Isaiah 9:7; 16:15; Jeremiah 23:5; Micah 4:7; Zechariah 9:10). John the Baptist and the prophets who preceded him collectively made it clear that the messiah would come to forgive us and restore us to God. He would come to bring righteousness and justice on earth, and to restore relationships and creation itself. He was to bring wholeness to all people. He was to be the Great Restorer.

This then was Jesus' core message. He speaks of the kingdom 37 times in the Gospel of Matthew alone. He must have announced it over and over again, probably at the start or finish of every proclamation moment. From town to town his message was the same. Matthew implies this, "From that time on Jesus began to preach, 'Repent, for the kingdom of heaven is near'" (Matthew 4:17; cf. Luke 4:43; 8:1).

He not only proclaimed the presence of the kingdom, but he used it as the subject matter of his teachings. In the Beatitudes, Jesus says, "*Blessed are the poor in spirit, for theirs is the kingdom of heaven.. . Blessed are those who are persecuted because of righteousness, for theirs is the kingdom of heaven*" (Matthew 5:3, 10). In his Sermon on the Mount, the kingdom was the subject that Jesus pivoted on as he addressed the matter of the law (Torah) and true righteousness (Matthew 5:19-21). Even most of his parables were cryptic illustrations of the kingdom from everyday life (Matthew 13).

The message of the kingdom was also what the disciples were commanded to proclaim. "*As you go, preach this message: 'The kingdom of heaven is near'* (Matthew 10:7; Luke 9:2; 10:9). There can be no question that for anyone serious about following Jesus, they must come to grips with the meaning of the kingdom of God.

The kingdom of God is the ruling presence of God ushered in by Jesus. It is God's will on earth as seen in the Hebrew parallelism of the Lord's Prayer: *Your kingdom come, your will be done.* The implication is that God's desire and will has not been occurring in our broken lives or fractured communities, but now it will—it must. The Great Restorer of all things is near. Right is coming to correct wrong, healing is coming to overcome sickness, justice is coming to right injustice, provision is coming to the poor and even animal and plant life is to be blessed (Isaiah 55:12). All that is broken on earth must be made whole in the presence of the king himself.

So What Did Jesus Mean?

The time has come. Whenever the prophets admonished the Israelites that their time had run out, the warning was apocalyptically ominous. This was a common expression in the New Testament as well (Galatians 4:4; Ephesians 1:10; 1 Timothy 2:6). Jesus is warning his hearers that the sand in the hourglass has completely dropped through. The messianic era has come. No more waiting, wondering or dilly-dallying. All that their souls have ever wanted is now here. But what is the kingdom of God?

Put simply, the kingdom of God is the ruling domain of God. It is the realm over which he is king and therefore his will is absolute. It is wonderful and fearful at once. On the one hand, it is wonderful because God is perfect and therefore he brings with him his flawless desire for love, truth, beauty and justice. On the other hand, it is fearful because those who resist God with their own willfulness will find conflict and eventually be judged. He doesn't bring a treaty or a throne to be shared. His brings his absolute divine rule.

This is the messianic promise from Isaiah 9:6-7:

> For to us a child is born, to us a son is given, and the government will be on his shoulders. And he will be called Wonderful Counselor, Mighty God, Everlasting Father, Prince of Peace. Of the increase of his government and peace there will be no end. He will reign on David's throne and over his kingdom, establishing and upholding it with justice and righteousness from that time on and forever. The zeal of the LORD Almighty will accomplish this.

But his reign is not fully accomplished; it is only *near*. What does Jesus mean by *near*? The literal is *it has come near*. Just as an advancing army sends out a messenger to arrange surrender, Jesus has come to prepare us for surrender. Jesus is the king incognito, appearing in advance of the invasion as a messenger: "Surrender, the invasion is at hand."

But the language avoids suggesting God's rule is beginning or has a starting point. His sovereign rule has always been, it never "begins." Nevertheless, to our rebel territory called earth, it is only near. God's *sovereign* rule has never left, but his *apparent* rule has been absent from this planet for a long time.

As children we would play a game of giving hints to someone looking for an object wearing a blindfold. When they drew closer to the object we would cry out "warmer, warmer." When they walked away from the object we would say "colder, colder." When they were on top of the object, almost touching it, we would shout out "hot!" Wholly Jesus is shouting out to us "hot!" To one man he even said, *You are not far from the kingdom of God* (Mark 12:34).

Time has run out and now we must decide—those who choose to continue their own self-healing will suffer the consequences. *He who seeks to save his life will lose it, but he who loses his life for my sake will find it* (Matthew 19:39).

WHAT WE HAVE HEARD

The hearers in Jesus' day tried to poke holes in Jesus and his message to conform him to their expectations. When Jesus announced in his own hometown that the promises of the kingdom were now fulfilled in his presence, they were furious and tried kill him, even though he grew up there (Luke 4:16-28). When he forgave sins he was called a blasphemer (Matthew 9:3). When he predicted his own death, Peter, his friend and follower, rebuked him, saying, "Never Lord." And when Jesus miraculously fed the thousands, they tried to return the favor by attempting to force him to become king (John 6:15). These people didn't want Wholly Jesus; they wanted a holey Jesus fit to their will.

This is still true today. Too often we want Jesus without his kingdom (his will), without his healing invasion. We want only a part of his will, not the whole package. We want forgiveness and heaven without interpersonal or intrapersonal transformation, without social or world transformation, and without personal sacrifice. The point is simple—we welcome Wholly Jesus' invasion but we still insist on fixing ourselves. We don't accept the whole package. This is not our surrender but our truce.

Instead of hearing Jesus' full message, we hear Jesus offer what we'd like to receive—forgiveness, acceptance, heaven and the end of suffering.

To have only part of Jesus' message is to know only a thin or holey Jesus; a Jesus who saves us from sin but forgets about serving others; a Jesus who saves our soul but not our body; a Jesus who judges culture but doesn't redeem it; a Jesus who gets people to church but doesn't get the church to the people; a Jesus who creates people with right doctrine and wrong lives; a Jesus who has grace for us but not for our enemies; a Jesus who cares about our country more than another; a Jesus who cares about forgiveness but not wholeness.

A thin Jesus is a reconstructed Jesus. A Jesus rebuilt by my denomination, country, church, political party, culture or subjective experience. The real Jesus is immense in person and agenda. He is unchanging. He is bigger than I know or than I can even imagine. Wholly Jesus invades.

If something is invasive, it moves beyond the comfortable boundaries of personhood, culture, society and religion. It is, in fact, beyond control. It is overtaking and overwhelming. Transformation, wholeness, salvation and healing on my terms are the precise reason why I am sinful and broken. Remedies that avoid transforming my volition are veneer at best. True transformation calls me to surrender with all my being. True wholeness requires an invasion and a takeover.

Keep in mind that the territories of our heart, our lives, our culture and world are already invaded with other agendas. It is not as though a void exists where there is the absence of any volition. We are filled with agendas that are often selfish, god-less and even at war with God's agenda (James 4). It is into this context that the agenda of God comes through Wholly Jesus.

Therefore our surrender—if it is to produce wholeness—must be holistic.

I often wonder if this is not why the church seems so anemic. Could it be that we present only a partial gospel and have only partial surrenders? Dallas Willard suggests this in *The Divine Conspiracy*.[5] An absolutely-right, partially-surrendered church in America, cloning itself over and over again, might do more harm than good. A church full of people who have received forgiveness and heaven, but retain the right to be selfish, hateful, divisive, greedy, etc., is extremely dangerous. We are to be the example and the product for anyone wondering what Wholly Jesus can do for a person's life.

Wherever the king is ruling with his nature (will), there is the kingdom of God—and this kingdom invades, overtakes and heals. The kingdom is not the church. The degree to which God's will is happening in that church is the degree to which his kingdom is present. However, the church may appear to be functioning just fine and the kingdom may be absent. The presence of the kingdom is as the tide; it ebbs and flows depending on the wholly surrender of his people to the king.

The kingdom (God's will) is brought to us through experience by the Spirit. And thus the *kingdom* is rarely mentioned in the Gospel of John. Instead he uses the language of the Spirit. We are to yield to the Counselor who brings God's presence to us. We are to allow him to make himself at home within us.

Perhaps our language has grown inadequate. "Accepting" Jesus does not do justice to the concept of the invading presence of the king. It makes us appear to be doing God a favor: "I have thought it over and I will accept you into my heart." It has the feeling of a truce or treaty. It's inherently different than a surrender.

I also question the location restriction we place on Jesus. He is invited into our *hearts*. This is wonderful if people understand their heart to be the throne ruling over the rest of their kingdom. But it's incomplete if it excludes our minds, our eyes, our bodies, our relationships, our occupations, our time, or our belongings. Heart Christianity creates a Docetic Christian (Docetism was a Gnostic heresy of the early church) who gives Jesus the spiritual part of his life and keeps all the physical, material aspects of their lives for themselves. As if Jesus moves into our hearts and abides there warmly but doesn't mess with our jobs, our cars, our houses, our families, our incomes, our relationships, etc. In order to receive the healing Wholly Jesus offers, we must surrender holistically, drawing no line between the spiritual and the physical or the sacred and the secular. If we surrender, we do so on his terms and his terms are all or nothing.

Inviting Jesus' Spirit into our lives is an important piece of the pie. But to limit his message to an invitation is to shrink Jesus to a party planner. Jesus does not merely say, "I invite you to heaven ... come celebrate with me one day." He says, "Instead, I invite you to become whole ... now and forever."

I prefer the concept of becoming a *follower of Jesus* to *becoming a Christian*. The first has motion and implies continued obedience while the latter is static and infers that a doctrinal box has been checked off—as if a ticket has been purchased. Plus, I don't know what the common listener thinks anymore when they hear the term Christian or what face they see when they hear the term. I want them to know that I have chosen to surrender, grabbing on to Jesus' hand

and walking with him. It is a life of complete surrender, knowing full well that only Jesus can make me whole.

The result of any reduction of Jesus' message is to end up with a very safe Jesus. The force of his message is then blunted and the invasion of this world through my life is prevented. He came to invade. We either prevent or propel his invasion.

A DECISIVE RESPONSE

For this reason, Jesus' invasion was followed by a simple yet pointed directive—*repent*. Sometimes the words were, *follow me*. A decisive response was requested. This does not undermine a process of learning and discovering Jesus. But once a person realized the king was here, decisiveness was next.

Wholly Jesus expected his followers to see the overwhelming value of the kingdom and take action accordingly: *"The kingdom of heaven is like treasure hidden in a field. When a man found it, he hid it again, and then in his joy went and sold all he had and bought that field* (Matthew 13:44). Something of great and obvious value demands an extravagant response.

The robust message of Jesus carried a strong sense of motion coming from heaven to earth. The content was about God's invading love, will and justice through Jesus. Jesus is the fulfillment of God's invasion, a transforming force that brought the rule (will, desire) of God into the moral center of a person's being. His coming was to prepare us for eternal life in the kingdom and to end the human mutiny against God. This kingdom was so valuable it was worth our lives, and many in Jesus' day were grabbing a hold of it with vigor (Luke 16:16).

We in the Western world of democracy are not used to hearing authoritative words such as *king, kingdom, advancing*. But we have read enough history and watched enough movies to understand. Jesus' language is revolutionary yet not forceful. Ultimately, we must choose to either surrender to the invasion of God's kingdom or put up a front.

There is no offer of a truce, no bartering. It is all or nothing with God. This is not the coming of the ice-cream man to your neighborhood, where you decide whether you will buy a frozen banana. It is not a solicitor who needs your support. It is not a politician who needs your vote. It is God's wholly will invading our planet, our lives, our hearts; and we ultimately must either surrender or suffer the eventual consequences of a broken world. We must pray, as Jesus did, *Your kingdom come, your will be done on earth as it is in heaven*.

There has never been a more powerful king, or a larger kingdom. There has never been a greater demand on the subjects of a kingdom. There has never been a greater promise of wholeness offered. This is the gospel. But is this the gospel we have heard?

Faith is a word that has been objectified into the term *doctrine* and we often think of faith as a doctrine hanging on a wall to which we give allegiance. But Soren Kierkegaard was right (along with Jon Hus, Martin Luther, John Wesley and George Whitefield). A personal, existential decision has been forced upon us and to believe is not a mere mental assent; it is a personal, trusting surrender of my whole being to the coming and commanding king. I cannot be born on earth a Christian; I must be reborn from above. I must personally decide whether I will entrust my domain to Jesus.

I must introspect and take an account of any troops inside of me; any pockets of resistance that still exist. We all have domains: family and friends, belongings, accomplishments and positions of influence. They are the domains over which we are the ruler, influencing with our broken, fallen will. The decision is to surrender it all to the king.

Jesus made this clear again and again, *if your right eye keeps you from following me, cut it out* (Matthew 5:29). *No one who takes up the plow and turns back is worthy of me* (Luke 9:62). *Let the dead bury the dead, follow me* (Matthew 8:22). *The one who finds the treasure, so values the treasure that he sells everything to obtain the treasure* (Matthew 13:44). *Sell all you have and give to the poor and follow me* (Mark 10:21).

Juan Ortiz, the author of a book called *Disciple*, used to tell the story of what it means to surrender to the king. He humorously says to God, "You're awfully demanding. I suppose the next thing you'll be wanting is my house." God responds, "Oh? You have a house? From now on the house is mine and you will live in it as guests and house others who need a place to stay." This dialogue continues with other belongings until it moves to the family.

"God, you're taking everything. I suppose the next thing you'll be asking for is my wife and children."

"Oh, you are married with children? From now on you will love them with my love and answer to me for how you treat them in my kingdom."[6]

Juan Ortiz captures well, in everyday terms, the intent of the kingdom of God. Believing with only my mind and not the things of my life is a heretical believing as much as legalism is heretical. The Bible knows nothing of believing as simply a mental assent. It only knows holistic believing that leads to full discipleship. And it is no coincidence that it is only through holistic surrender that we will be made whole.

***

When I first became a follower, I was given a copy of the Living Bible New Testament. I devoured it. Even though it was finals week in my first year of college, I could not put the book down. In three days I was done. I couldn't believe that the truth of these words had existed all around me for 18 years and I had never read them. The words of Jesus struck me as wonderfully severe.

I surrendered all I had used to find significance and identity. For me it was my rock music and the bands I had played in. I took stock of what I had at the age of 18. I didn't have much, only musical instruments. So I took my Vox organ, my Fender Coronado II guitar and Super Reverb amplifier down to the church and said, "Here, it's yours," and walked away. I needed something that was decisive in my life, something that tangibly expressed the holistic surrender of my heart.

The beautiful irony was that a year later I was at a church retreat. The worship band was playing and said they needed a keyboard player to help them, so I eagerly walked to the stage. To my surprise, there was my old organ and amplifier waiting for my fingers to play. So much of life is this way. It is not that God needs the things we surrender, it is that we need to be set free from the stuff that wraps its tentacles around our hearts. In reality Jesus promised, *"No one who has left home or brothers or sisters or mother or father or children or fields for me and the gospel will fail to receive a hundred times as much in this present age (homes, brothers, sisters, mothers, children and fields—and with them, persecutions) and in the age to come, eternal life* (Mark 10:29-30).

Nevertheless, now that I am 35 years older it is much more difficult to think of giving away my things. The lesson, however, is no less clear: surrendering to the invading kingdom applies to all of my life. If it only applies to your soul and heaven, what cost is there? Who wouldn't raise their hand and go forward, if the surrender is simply that you continue to do what you want and God will give you heaven. Without the kingdom message of invasion, Wholly Jesus can be and has been greatly thinned out.

The invasion has begun and those who are a part of his kingdom experience an internal transformation and are part of an external transformation, bringing Jesus' life, love and truth to culture around us. It is time for us to burn our castles and enter the invading kingdom. The church has been a castle in the woods for far too long.

chapter six

Wholly Jesus in a Material World

It is no use walking anywhere to preach unless our walking is our preaching.

— St. Francis of Assisi

T he moment was awkward for his disciples. Some had previously followed the ascetic preacher called the Baptist. Now they were with their new rabbi, Jesus, at their first social function—a wedding. Being Jewish, all of the disciples had been to multiple bar mitzvahs and weddings. They knew how to laugh and celebrate with the best of them. But now they were together with Jesus. Unsure of his attitude toward such merriment, they remained silent, watching for his lead.

Suddenly Jesus' mother, Mary, approached him and whispered, "They have no more wine."

"Why is she telling Jesus this," the disciples thought to themselves. "She's acting as if he should take responsibility for the celebration. Why would Jesus care if the party goes on?"

With firm tenderness he responded, "Dear woman, why do you involve me?"

"There, I guess that put her in her place," the disciples silently mused.

But like a good Jewish mother, Mary was relentless and told the attending servants nearby, "Do whatever my son tells you."

Now the servants and the disciples were curious. Jesus said nothing but his eyes were looking at six large water jugs, used for the ceremonial washing of the guests' hands and feet. They were no small
ceramic pitchers, and while now empty, each one earlier held 20-30
gallons of water. The silence was broken as Jesus spoke to the servants, pointing to the jars, "Fill the jars with water."

"What is Jesus thinking," the disciples pondered. "Is he going to
sober up the party with some illustration about ceremonial water?"
Once again, the disciples wisely said nothing, listening with their eyes.

Once the jars were filled to the brim, which took some time, Jesus
spoke to servants once more: "Now draw some out and take it to the
master of the banquet." The servants quickly obeyed.

"What is he doing? Is Jesus just going to serve the master of the
banquet water?" the disciples questioned. "That will douse the wedding's fire for sure."

In silent fear the disciples cringed to hear what the master's reaction would be. "What? He seems to like what he's tasting…"

The banquet host stood up from his middle-eastern, reclining
position, motioning to everyone that he wanted to make an
announcement. Raising his chalice toward the bridegroom, he shout-
ed out, "Everyone brings out the choice wine first and then the
cheaper wine after the guests have had too much to drink; but you
have saved the best for now."

This was the first of Jesus' miracles. His were earthy, humble,
without-fanfare miracles that pointed to his nature. Feeding the five
thousand, walking on water, calming the winds and waves, healing the
sick and raising the dead were still to come. But, never were these
works of power done in a showy, presumptuous way. Never with a
flashy magic wand, an "abracadabra" or a puff of purple smoke. Many
of them were quite private and many times he asked the one who was
healed to tell no one. He was no illusionist. His miracles were calm,
natural and performed within an earthly context: through his voice,
his hands, his saliva, the mud, and also through the words and actions
of his disciples.

The Apostle John, reflecting on these years with Jesus and his
unique incarnate style, wrote, *"That which was from the beginning,*

which we have heard, which we have seen with our eyes, which we have looked at and our hands have touched—this we proclaim concerning the Word of life" (1 John 1:1). The Creator, who made the world and made us from clay, had come to redeem the world and its inhabitants physically, not merely spiritually.

Thinking of Jesus' first miracle always reminds me of my first ethnic wedding in Boston. Many guests were first and second generation immigrants from Europe. Boy, did they know how to celebrate. Laughter, dancing and music like I had never seen at even a rock show. The high point of the celebration was when the mother of the groom was hoisted on a chair and six groomsmen struggled to dance around with her on their shoulders. She was a good 280 pounds of jostling joy and such fun!

It still makes me wonder about my view of God, my understanding of salvation, and my freedom to celebrate within my humanity. Did I have a God that entered my humanity that way? I had a God who forgave me of my sins, waits for me in heaven, and told me to stay away from anything too fun because it might lead to sin. Was the incarnate God, Wholly Jesus, truly that earthy? Would my Jesus turn water into wine, if only to continue—even elevate—the celebration?

THE BEAUTY OF A BROKEN BODY IN A MATERIAL WORLD

Very few people woke up this morning wondering how to get their sins forgiven or how to get into heaven. Some did, thank God, but not many. But millions, if not billions, were awakened in angst about how to fix some part of their lives. They went out the door, grabbed the phone, bought a book or did a computer search on how to heal their checkbook, their marriage, their children, their illness or their torn mind. It is not that forgiving of sins and heaven are unimportant—not at all. They are of the utmost importance. It's just not what most people were thinking about when they opened their eyes this morning.

The same was true in Jesus' day. The vast majority of those who approached Jesus were concerned about some physical need. It varied amongst health, relationships, provision, mobility and finances.

We are earthy people made of the earth. We live in time and space; we eat food from the ground; we have to make a living with mental and physical energy; we communicate audibly with our voices; we only see physical things; we touch, smell, taste and hear; we procreate by intersecting our bodies; and new humans come out of our bodies. We are utterly physical beings. Yet, God is Spirit. So how do we approach him? How does he invade us?

Much of the Western and Eastern tendency in religion has been to minimize or overcome the physical aspect of life as if it were a hindrance or even a negative. At funerals we sometimes speak of the body as if it was a cage that entrapped the soul. In the West, Greek philosophy has greatly influenced our view of the material world. We see it as Plato or the Gnostics did—either something to put up with until we get to heaven, or worse, something quite negative and morally disconnected from the spiritual.

The Hebrews, to the contrary, uniquely lived their spirituality as something that was viewed, appreciated and understood within the physical confines. They viewed God as entering this material world with redemptive motives. Their sacrifices were feasts with God—not merely prayers. Their nearness to God was translated into daily civic life. While the direction and emphasis of most religions points from earth to heaven, the arrow of Hebrew spirituality points from heaven to earth—"Thy kingdom come."

It was into this culture that Jesus came, turning water into real wine and celebrating at a noisy, festive wedding. His miracles were physical: the walking on water, the multiplying of the loaves and fish—even his own resurrection. He even proved his resurrection by consuming fish.

The Western church has tended to minimize the physical and emphasize the important yet intangibles of forgiveness and heaven. It has often been taught, or implied through emphasis, that the needs of the body are not as important as the needs of the soul. That earth is not as important as heaven. That emotion should be ignored or suppressed. That finances, relationships, employment, social acceptance, justice and physical health are not nearly as important as our spiritual health. This portrait of spirituality—of following Wholly Jesus—is vastly different from the one in the gospels.

Admittedly, there are a few verses that place a priority on the soul when weighed against physical persecution and physical wealth (Matthew 10:28; 16:26). And in truth, our soul outlives our body. However, the Scripture is strong to emphasize that we receive new physical bodies (1 Corinthians 15). Scripture knows nothing of Christians floating on clouds with harps. Rather, the overall avalanche of Scripture leans in a holistic direction that sees all of life as spiritual. God's kingdom comes to invade all of life—our whole life—including the physical. Even our redeemed future will include a new physical heaven and a new physical earth.[1] To be sure, consider how Jesus approached the physical side of life.

WHAT JESUS PRIMARILY DID

In a few instances in the gospels, we are given summary statements about Jesus' earthly ministry. Matthew tells us for example, *Jesus went throughout Galilee, teaching in their synagogues, preaching the good news of the kingdom, and healing every disease and sickness among the people* (Matthew 4:23). Five chapters later Matthew makes another summary comment, *Jesus went through all the towns and villages, teaching in their synagogues, preaching the good news of the kingdom and healing every disease and sickness* (Matthew 9:35). Peter's summary found in the Book of Acts is, *how God anointed Jesus of Nazareth with the Holy Spirit and power, and how he went around doing good and healing all who were under the power of the devil, because God was with him* (Matthew 10:38). It is clear that on a regular basis, from town to town, Jesus, the itinerant Messiah, regularly taught, proclaimed and physically healed people. This behavior was in clear contrast to John the Baptist's behavior, a man who only preached and baptized (according the gospels and Josephus). Jesus' ministry touched, cared for and healed the whole person, not just the soul.

His recorded healings and miracles are no small part of the gospels. According to Morton Kelsey's tabulation, there are 41 distinct healings recorded in the four gospels. Eight that might be categorized as deliverance or exorcism from an evil spirit, in two instances lepers were healed (one included 10 at once), nine instances of various types of unnamed healings among very large crowds, six healings of physical deformities, three resurrections from the dead and many other healings including at least seven of blindness and deafness.[2] There is no question that Jesus was viewed as a healer of the body.

One of Jesus' first healings was of a man with Hansen's Disease— a.k.a. leprosy. In 1st century Israel, leprosy was viewed as a deadly, contagious disease and there was no choice but to ostracize those suffering into leper homes and colonies. No leper was allowed to intermingle with the normal population. So to have leprosy was both a physical deformity that led to death, and also a social stigma that isolated the person from normal life. Leprosy was a physical, emotional, social and spiritual blight.

"Lord," the man said, "if you want to, you can make me well again." The leper is saying the only thing that stands in the way of his wholeness is Jesus' willingness to heal. Jesus quickly puts away all doubt, perhaps with a smile and a twinkle in his eye, and says, "I want to." (Luke 5:13, NLT).

This willingness of Jesus to heal is something the church needs to hear today, loud and clear. We are guilty of doubting the goodness of God. We too often assume he is intentionally inflicting us with pain because, "He wants to teach us something." We too easily acquiesce to the assumption that a broken body is our "cross to bear." We often pray for healing but with "thy will be done." When he has already made it clear—"I am willing." An unwilling God is directly built on dualism.

Obviously, not everyone we pray for is healed, but neither is everyone we witness to "saved." When another is not healed, we say it was God's will—yet we would never say it was not God's will to save them. Certainly, we don't know God's ways, his timings, his methodology and the extent of the exponential brokenness of the world. But we must agree that he is good and willing and his entire mission in coming was to heal and save. He did not come to maim, injure or divide, yet well-meaning Christians convinced of the sovereignty of God have not merged the sovereign image with the wholly image of the invading king who still remains absolutely good.

After healing the centurion's servant and then healing Peter's mother-in-law of her fever, Jesus spends the rest of the evening healing dozens of people (Matthew 8). On into the night, though weary, he has compassion for the sick. His compassion is no less than that of the centurion who was worried about his servant.

Jesus is moved with compassion and understanding, not judgment. "The most important reason that Jesus healed was that he cared about people and suffered when they did... Jesus so loved that he healed."[3]

Author Morton Kelsey gives us several common misconceptions about why Jesus healed. One is that God just likes to make people so sick and then heal them to get their attention. In other words, "Now that I have your attention and you are listening... Be healed." To whatever degree God does this directly or indirectly, one would have to agree that this is not the picture of Jesus in the Gospels and therefore plays a small role in the believer's life. Paul does experience God that way regarding the thorn in his flesh, but that appears to be the exception on the rule (2 Corinthians 12:7).

Another misconception given for Jesus' healings is that they are to demonstrate how we, too, might heal the sick. The gospel stories then become sort of a how-to manual for healing. Perhaps there is a slight example of this modeled when Peter raises Dorcas from the dead (Acts 9:39). Peter seems to imitate some of Jesus' behavior found in Mark 5:41. But whatever methodology we learn from Jesus' healings, we must beware. Our actions and words must ultimately be connected to faith in the person of Jesus. Our trust is not in learned behavior. Magic trusts in the right words and behaviors to control the elements. Scripture is against all forms of magic. In Jesus, we do not learn the magic of healing or the right methodology. The Apostle James' simple primitive approach to healing relies on simple faith and prayer, not technique. Our confidence must not remain in how to speak, use one's hands, keep one's eyes closed, or how to shake. Simple faith is all we must know.

Another common misconception given for Jesus' healings is that they are only there to point to "salvation" (forgiveness and heaven).

This line of thought assumes that if those healed are not converted, the healing was in vain. Kelsey wisely notes that, "This idea completely ignores the fact that healings actually occurred, and that they were effective in bringing new life right then as well as in confirming the expectation of life to come. Essentially everything we know of Jesus of Nazareth underlines the importance of this present life..." not just the future.[4]

Finally, some Christians think Jesus' healings were merely signs. That is, healings are not acts of compassion, but rather, pointers to his person and power. Yet, Jesus often told people to tell no one. Jesus, in fact, rejected the attention and the concept of signs. He said the only sign that you will receive is the sign of Jonah (Matthew 12:39).

The practical conclusions about the reason for "Jesus' healing was that he was the son of God, filled with the Spirit of God and fully expressing God's nature for men."[5] He cared about the value and dignity of people made in the image of God. He was hostile toward the brokenness he saw in people and society. Sickness hampered people "in being what they ought to be and he wanted them to have life and that abundantly."[6] When Wholly Jesus invades, physical transformation begins.

From Jesus' ministry, we learn three things about our material world. First, God is opposed to sickness. Whatever we want to say about God's "permissive" or "temporal will" will regarding his use of sickness, we must understand that he is flatly against it. He and his kingdom are always moving toward wholeness.

Second, the health of the mind, soul and body in Christianity cannot be easily separated, if at all. Jesus didn't try, and neither should the church. It is dangerous for us to second-guess God's sovereignty and hypothesize reasons why God wants people sick. We should be in motion toward restoring people as bio-psycho-socio-spiritual beings while always restoring their relationship with God through forgiveness in Christ.

Third and finally, Jesus' followers are to carry on the ministry of Jesus. It is clear that he gave his disciples the same ministry as his own (Mark 6:7; Matthew 10:5-8; Luke 9:1), and that the church equally took on his mantle. Jesus' ministry was to preach, teach and heal.

Whereas he represented the Father to us, we represent Jesus to others. But ours is also a holistic ministry as was his. It's not a truncated ministry that only deals with the immaterial soul.

It would be wrong to make ourselves only doctors of the soul; that kind of dualism is not available to us from the gospels. As followers of Jesus, we don't want to find ourselves fighting against things for which Jesus' ministry exists. A quick glance at Jesus' continual response to sickness cannot help but attract us to his compassionate power. Whether it is the ten lepers who are healed of their disease and social abuse, or the man with the withered hand that Jesus boldly heals on the Sabbath, time and time again, Jesus is unhesitant to heal. Wholeness is his mantra and we must imitate him in this way.

THE BLINDERS TO WHOLLY JESUS: MODERNITY AND DUALISM

Our present world has resisted the view of a holistic Jesus. Two primary influences have restricted our perception: modernity and dualism. Modernity (post Enlightenment) has restricted our knowledge spectrum to only include that which seems reasonable (rationalism) and that which is scientifically verifiable (empiricism). All other forms of knowledge are discounted, including intuition and revelation. It's as if modernity arbitrarily decided that only two colors of the rainbow exist.

When this notion spills into culture, the result is a cold, grey naturalism. This is the belief that our world is a closed system and that God (if he does exist) does not invade our world supernaturally to communicate and perform miracles. It is clear that miracles and modernity do not mix. Modernity became the bully of the playground who forced religion, philosophy, history and the behavioral sciences to tow the line. Thomas Jefferson applied this "enlightened" naturalistic perspective to his personal copy of the New Testament by removing all miracles and keeping only Jesus' moral teachings.

Similarly, Western dualism has split the physical and the spiritual realm. Starting with Plato, continuing through Gnosticism, and on into Cartesian philosophy, dualism has dominated the landscape of Western thought for centuries. But the end result in the 20th century was to hand over the material world to science and commerce, and to give religion the leftovers—the denigrated or ridiculed spiritual and metaphysical realm. The consequence of dualism for religion in a material world is irrelevancy.

One example of the effects of dualism is found in psychology, a discipline named after the *soul*. It quickly redefined itself as the science of the *self*. Monism (the idea that only the material world exists) dominated the behavioral era of psychology.

Another example is found in the life of ministers. Every pastor has felt this imposed irrelevancy when visiting a patient in a hospital. Normally when a medical doctor walks into the room, the pastor yields to that person who takes care of the body.

Unfortunately, much of the Western church has retreated into this spiritual realm, yielding the important, physical world to the "experts." As a result, the church remains silent about physical things like health, poverty, human injustice and the care of the planet, but continues to grow louder and louder about the soul. There appears, of course, to be a reversing of this trend, but the current is strong and the majority of Christian churches still get pulled into this mold.

The problem with a church that only accents the spiritual is not only theological, but also practical. We end up with a church that is so heavenly minded, it's no earthly good. We have a church which retreats from the poor, from injustices, from the sick, from hurting marriages and families, and from caring for the planet. Or perhaps a church that picks and chooses its physical concerns. The church has often chosen to be involved in only material issues that directly affect it or its congregation. So the suburban church fights abortion, drugs and the definition of marriage. Meanwhile the urban church fights poverty, gangs and loss of its male role models. But both lack an integrated, holistic picture of salvation. Wholeness is neither suburban nor urban.

Only now, in this postmodern era, are things changing. Although post modernity has its own set of problems, dualism is dying along with the reign of rationalism and empiricism.   Some ministers, churches and temples are gaining physical credibility again. Soul is a popular term again within the mainstream. Since Thomas Moore's

Care of the Soul, dozens of popular books have been written about the soul. Empirical studies have defended the efficacy of prayer, meditation and spiritual care for hospital patients.[7] Secular hospitals are hiring chaplains. Religious institutions in the material world are again doing something physical about the brokenness all around us. We are beginning to join Wholly Jesus in making things whole again.

Still, in this brackish water, the shadow of modernity lingers. Within the church, teachers and scholars often don't know what to do with a miraculous and healing Jesus. The more liberal scholars still blatantly yield to modernity, deciding that the supernatural events never happened. But more disconcerting are the covert conservative responses to the lordship of modernity. For example, instead of studying and enjoying the stunning miracles of Jesus, many make apologies or excuses for the miracles. Some argue that the audience Jesus taught was full of poor, illiterate, simple people who would not understand intelligent presentations, only "signs and wonders." Obviously, they say, Jesus' poor audience was not enlightened as we are today. Others maintain that there were utilitarian reasons as to why Jesus performed these miracles, primarily to exhibit social acceptance of those who were outcasts from religion because of their disease. There is no doubt these reasons may have some validity, but they must be secondary not primary. If the shadow of modernity is to be removed, we must accept that the glaring reason for Jesus' healings is to exhibit the redemptive, loving, wholly nature of God.[8]

To be sure, those who use healings or miracles in a flamboyant, showy way to build their own narcissistic empires must be suspect, just as we are suspicious of those who use sermons or their positions to build their own kingdom. And unbiblical theologies about healing, such as "naming and claiming" healing and wealth, must be countered with good theology, just as we must with any teaching in any discipline. Ultimately, we must applaud any part of the church that is moving the kingdom forward holistically: not merely spiritually, but also physically.

One might argue that our experience has largely dictated our preference of the immaterial over the material in the church. We see people receive Christ into their hearts more than we see people physically healed. We are simply pragmatic. We gravitate toward what works. The unseen seems to work, while the visible world is a difficult place to be successful.

Yet, the New Testament is, perhaps inconveniently for many, Jewish and is therefore all about the physical, tangible love of God in and through real people. It never promotes theoretical love. God's love in the New Testament is a verb, filled with sacrificial action.

Jesus kept this pace by commanding us to love him with all our heart, soul, mind and strength (Matthew 22:37). Later the Apostles Paul and John carry on this strong holistic approach: *May your whole spirit, soul and body be kept blameless at the coming of our Lord Jesus Christ* (1 Thessalonians 5:23); *Dear friend, I pray that you may enjoy good health and that all may go well with you, even as your soul is getting along well* (3 John 2).

What if the true Jesus is extremely concerned about the physical? What if his priority is to redeem us whole and it's not only OK but fabulous to be physically human?

JESUS' HOLISTIC, SEAMLESS APPROACH

One of the most startling of Jesus' stories is the healing of the paralytic. It is filled with intrigue, tension, humor and an amazing conclusion. Luke tells it best. Jesus is teaching inside a home; it may have even been his rented headquarters or Peter's home in Capernaum on the shore of the lake. According to Matthew, Jesus had just crossed the lake in a boat.

While Jesus teaches, the crowd swells, packing the house, and spills out onto the street. Among the crowd are the religious referees, the Pharisees and teachers of the Torah. They are there to see if Jesus stays on the playing field of their orthodoxy or if he steps out of bounds, which he was infamous for doing.

While he's teaching, a group of four men arrive to the house carrying their paralyzed friend on a stretcher. They immediately realize they will never get through the crowd. They become desperate.

With the kind of ingenuity we all love, the men get creative and resourceful. They climb up to the outdoor patio where families slept and ate on warm summer nights. There they begin to bore a hole through the roof. First the tiles are chipped away, and then they begin to dig through the adobe base. At some point, stuff begins to fall on the heads of those sitting below. They try to scoot back to avoid the shower of dust and debris, but there isn't room. Finally, the disturbance causes Jesus to stop teaching and look up.

The crowd sees the tip of a stretcher peak through the hole in the roof and then the feet of a man tied to the stretcher by a rope. With another rope the four men above lower their friend. He hovers in mid-air right in front of Jesus. The crowd pushes back even more to make room as the man finally rests on the floor. The people erupt with applause and cheers.

Jesus smiles, then laughs with the people as he looks at the man and then scans the faces of those sitting and standing. His eyes meet the Pharisees and the teachers. Then with a face of compassion and a twinkle in his eye, he takes one step toward the man and speaks.

"Friend," he says. "Your sins are forgiven." Some gasp at his words, but most are still silent as the religious leaders turn to each other with furrowed brows and shaking heads. They all know what the other is thinking but not saying, "Only God can forgive sins." This is blasphemy!

Jesus turns from the man to the religious referees, who have thrown their yellow flags on the field. "Why are you thinking these things in your hearts? Which is easier: to say, 'Your sins are forgiven,' or to say, 'Get up and walk?' But that you may know that the Son of Man has authority on earth to forgive sins..." He pauses and now turns back to the paralyzed man, "I tell you, get up, take your mat and go home" (Luke 5:22-24).

The healing was instant. The man stood up. The miracle was not simply the healing of the paralysis, but of the atrophy of muscles and the lack of learned balance. As the crowd gasped, the man stood before them. "They were all filled with awe."

Then welcoming the man back into responsible society Jesus said to him, "Now gather up your stretcher and go home." And he did so in full view of everyone. The crowd roused to an ovation and filled the room with "Hallelujahs!"

Here we see Jesus physically bringing the kingdom of redemption to a paralyzed man. We don't know the cause or how long he had been paralyzed, but we do know much of 1st century Jewish society. It's likely that the religious leaders considered him a sinner because they believed bad things only happened to bad people. Therefore, the synagogue may have even excommunicated him. Fortunately, this man still had some friends to help him. His responsible income was gone and there was no workman's compensation or social security. He was unable to dress himself, perhaps even to feed himself. He was dependent on others for survival. And he was left in his brokenness of sin, physical disability and mental anguish. Every part of his life was seismically broken.

Although the Pharisees parsed spiritual brokenness (sin) from the physical paralysis, Jesus saw it all as one and moved holistically to redeem the man. Not only does he show forgiveness and heal the man, he goes further to welcome the man back into society by allowing him to pick up his own stretcher and carry it home. Anyone who had been disabled for sometime knows the ultimate joy is to be able to do things for oneself again. Wholly Jesus even gave him back his dignity.

chapter seven

Mangers, Mustard Seeds, Children & Crosses

I learned that it is better, a thousand-fold, for a proud man to fall and be humbled than to hold up his head in his pride and fancied innocence. I learned that he that will be a hero, will barely be a man.

— Leo Tolstoy

I hid in the bookstore for almost an hour. Pretending to be interested in the books, I peered out the window to see if it was safe. The two secret-service-looking men with dark suits and sunglasses continued to hover around my car.

Earlier I had driven onto the large campus of a Christian outreach organization to purchase a book for a friend from their bookstore on my way to meet him for lunch. But upon my arrival, cars occupied all of the parking stalls except for the one marked "reserved" for the well-known president of the organization. Being young and in a hurry, I decided to park my Subaru in his stall. "He's probably never here any way," I muttered to myself to excuse my behavior.

While I was in the bookstore I saw the shiny maroon, boat-sized Oldsmobile pull up and block the back of my car. Three men in dark suits and sunglasses jumped out and began to buzz like bees around my dirty gray car. Finally, one of the men opened the backdoor of the Oldsmobile and out popped the one—the famous president of this

Christian organization. "Oh no!" I said under my breath. "What do I do?"

As the important man was escorted into the office building, the other two lingered to catch the insolent peon who dared to park his car in the president's spot. I knew I had two possibilities: walk out and surrender to these powerful temple guards or make my great escape.

My internal debate was ended when the two men guarding my car walked inside, leaving the large expensive car to block mine from backing up and exiting. I guess they figured that now no one would be able to leave without asking the maroon carrier to move. They were wrong, but I had to act quickly.

I hurried out of the bookstore and slid into my car. I slammed it into four-wheel drive and climbed over the curb in front of me onto the 10-foot-wide grass island and off the other side. I then raced the half-mile to the front gate hoping that no one would radio the gate-keeper to block the gate. No one had. With my heart racing, I had escaped.

My behavior was juvenile at best, I know, but to be honest, I relish the story. I have always questioned the reserved parking stalls—and anything of special attention—for those of God's kingdom. I can understand this in the mainstream world, but it's often built on the "king of the mountain" game and seems to go against so much of what Jesus taught and did. On the contrary, Wholly Jesus seemed to promote a hidden, inverted world where servants are more important than kings, mangers are more glorious than thrones, mustard seeds are mightier than Roman armies ... and people are more important than parking spaces.

As children, we can easily imagine a world upside down from our own. One where we can walk on ceilings, defy gravity and even fly. We are captivated by the intricate worlds of *Alice and Wonderland* or *The Matrix*, where everything is the opposite of what we intuitively expect. When we are young, these things are possible. What happens when we grow older?

Jesus' explanations of the kingdom seem like the description of an upside down world—like a world only a child can so easily believe. The uniqueness of this kingdom is that its values and methodology are the inversion of the kingdoms of this world—the opposite of what we know and see. For Wholly Jesus, up is down and down is up.

THE NATURE OF JESUS

If you've ever wondered what Jesus' personality was like, it can be partially inferred by a portion of a verse in Matthew 12:16: he warned them not to tell who he was. Here Jesus had healed many sick people and afterwards he strictly requested that they not broadcast his identity. How curious ... and this was not the only occasion.

He continually told people not to tell others who he was or what he had done (Mark 3:12; 7:36; 8:30; 9:9). This is not the way celebrities or power brokers behave in our societies. In our king-of-the-mountain world, people declare their own greatness and do not think for a moment to hush the crowds buzzing about them. If anyone was worthy of attention, greatness and notoriety, it was Jesus. Yet he would not promote himself. He was to become the most influential man to have ever lived and yet he often told others to keep quiet about him.

The theological answer is that Jesus wasn't yet finished with his ministry and wasn't yet ready to die. He didn't want to bring to himself too much attention, making the religious leaders in Jerusalem jealous. He wanted at least three years to invest his life in the disciples and make his message clear. There's no doubt this is true, but Matthew actually does some of his own interpreting here and tells us why he thinks Jesus did what he did.

Matthew points us to Jesus' nature. Quoting Isaiah 42:3, he explains that the messiah was to be controlled by a different set of values than we commonly find in the leaders of this world:

> "Here is my servant whom I have chosen, the one I love, in whom I delight; I will put my Spirit on him, and he will proclaim justice to the nations. He will not quarrel or cry out; no one will hear his voice in the streets. A bruised reed he will not break, and a smoldering wick he will not snuff out, till he leads justice to victory." (Matthew 12:18-20)

Here, Matthew is confirming that Jesus is the messiah who has come to champion full justice to the whole world, bringing holistic salvation in every way. But he will do it in a unique, counterintuitive way. He will not be loud or come with a darn-right attitude, nor will he force himself upon anyone. Rather, he will be so humble, gentle and compassionate that the broken person who feels like the bruised reed, or the hopeless person who feels like a smoldering wick, will connect with him as an advocate and receive the justice he brings.

It was this same quality of gentleness and compassion that endeared God toward the first king David. As a shepherd-boy, David defended the lambs from the bear and the lion. It was this quality that allowed Nathan the prophet to provoke David to repentance after his sins of adultery and murder. Nathan described a man who brazenly took advantage of a poor family by using their pet lamb for a barbeque. David immediately realized and confessed he had been "that man" who had taken advantaged of the poor "bruised reed," and consequently repented. This combination of strength and tenderness is rare, but ever so attractive.

But this is not the image of leadership we are used to in this world. Is it possible for a leader to serve this way? Is it possible for servanthood to cohabitate with strength and leadership? Our CEOs, team captains and politicians are often grandiose, dominant and self-serving. Narcissism is even rampant in the pulpits of America. Could it be that the value structure of this world—the king-of-the-mountain world that we know and have come to accept—is actually a broken inversion of the kingdom of God? Perhaps the power/control paradigm of this world is different than Jesus' paradigm. Perhaps in the unbroken world, servants really were greatest.

UP IS DOWN, DOWN IS UP—THE BEATITUDES

From the manger to the cross, Jesus consistently presented an upside down paradigm toward leadership, character and the kingdom as a whole. In the Sermon on the Mount, in his miracles, in his parables and in his indictments of the religious leaders, Jesus, without varying, promoted the servant and the poor. In his incarnation and crucifixion, he modeled the meaning of his kingdom.

Right out of the gate in the Sermon on the Mount, Jesus turned our pyramidal top-down world on its head. In the Beatitudes he singles out the poor, the hungry, the thirsty and the persecuted as heroes of the kingdom. In the remainder of the sermon, Jesus differentiates between the false spirituality that proudly advances one's ego verses true authentic discipleship. Humility and authenticity are key characteristics in Jesus and his kingdom.

Wholly Jesus makes it clear that those who lie at the bottom of the socio-economic food chain are really at the top in his kingdom. Matthew calls them "poor in spirit," while Luke simply refers to them as "poor." Certainly poverty has a way of breaking a person's spirit— but from a kingdom worldview those broken by poverty are blessed. Contrary to the way society treats the underprivileged, the poor are honored in the kingdom of God.

In the other Beatitudes this upside down world is reinforced. Blessed are those who mourn and those who are meek. This humility and brokenness is reminiscent of the writings of the first king David: *"The sacrifices of God are a broken spirit; a broken and contrite heart, O God, you will not despise"* (Psalm 51:17). These are the values of Jesus' kingdom. Humility is the ammunition of the kingdom of God.

By contrast this world's system honors the proud and the aggressive. But Jesus' words are spoken in a religious context. We exalt people who pose behind their position and their possessions, as well as those who stand next to people perceived to be important. We admire those who have beauty, brains or bucks. We honor the king of the mountain. It is the paradigm of power and control. As the old southern saying goes, "Them who have, get."

I've noticed that the power/control paradigm rules in religion, too. I was at a Pastor's Conference this week. Pastors, like anyone else, can strut like peacocks fanning their feathers to indicate the size of the church membership, their budget, their books and their new building. Often the pastors of importance have an entourage of servants and pastors of smaller churches running alongside asking questions.

This is certainly true in the entertainment world. Everyone knows who is at the top of the charts. There is a pecking order that is dictated by spins and record sells. The Hollywood handshake is the same as the pastoral handshake – and those with the biggest entourage hold the most power.

I've discovered something about my own heart and when I meet a stranger is the best time to find out what I pose and posture behind. When I'm asked, "Pastor, how big is your church? Tell me about your book. Where have you recently traveled? Are you on the radio?" How I answer those questions or steer the conversation reveals much about my heart. Do I serve, as Os Guinness asks, an audience of One?[1]

HUMILITY AND AUTHENTICITY ARE RELATED

In the remainder of Jesus' Sermon on the Mount, he reinforces the fact that the kingdom is comprised of authentic people who are increasingly whole, not posers of importance. "For I tell you that unless your righteousness surpasses that of the Pharisees and the teachers of the law, you will certainly not enter the kingdom of heaven" (Matthew 5:20). His followers' righteousness must exceed that of the professionally trained, religious elite.

Jesus knows that it is common to use religion for pride or self-righteousness, but if you're going to go in that direction then you won't be in God's kingdom. Humility and authenticity are not so distant cousins. The transformation of a kingdom citizen can't be one of veneer, of learned behavior, but one of depth, of true character. The process of becoming whole is not a process of distinction, but of integration into the Whole.

Jesus continues in the Sermon on the Mount saying, *"Not everyone who says to me, 'Lord, Lord,' will enter the kingdom of heaven, but only he who does the will of the Father who is in heaven"* (Matthew 7:21). Jesus warns us against using the things of God for our prideful ends. Toward the end of his ministry he warns us again *"Woe to you, teachers of the law and Pharisees, you hypocrites! You are like whitewashed tombs, which look beautiful on the outside but on the inside are full of dead men's bones and everything unclean"* (Matthew 23:27). To be in the presence of God should produce humility, a sweet sense of wholeness and authenticity of person. To wear God like makeup violates everything. We are simply to become his reflection, not a distinct person with our own face.

Wholly Jesus' followers are to become integrated humans. So Jesus gives us a series of examples of integration and authenticity: *"You have heard that it was said to the people long ago, 'Do not ... But I tell you ...* (Matthew 5:21, 27, 33, 43)." In these examples he challenges the common veneer religion. Faithfulness, relationship harmony, honesty, justice and love are not just surface behaviors. Jesus raises the bar to authentic spirituality by placing his finger on the intention, not just the outward behavior. He clarifies that true fidelity disallows lust not just adultery, true harmony excludes hate not just murder, true honesty requires integrity not just religious vows, true justice requires mercy not simply fairness, and true love is for your enemy not just your friends.

The religious model of the day demonstrated the lack of integration and transformation while providing Jesus with a clear-cut contrast to the invading kingdom. The Pharisees were dis-integrated hypocrites. Jesus' command to be perfect as God is, can be understood in this regard. It means to be whole, to be integrated in word, intent and deed. Be the real deal. He is not arguing for perfectionism; he is asking for a holistic, integrated, authentic approach to discipleship and it is a clear indictment against the religious posers of his day... and ours.

What counts is a God-centered, transformed, integrated life; becoming who God designed you to be. This is common sense. It doesn't matter how fancy your suit is if there's no money in your wallet. It doesn't matter how flashy your car is if there's no engine under the hood. It doesn't matter how loud your prayer is if there's no God in your heart. The world understands these associations. So Jesus says, "Don't use my stuff to advance your ego." Up is down.

HOBBITS OF THE KINGDOM

I think J.R.R. Tolkien best captured this upside-down world of the kingdom when he made little hobbits the rock stars of his stories.

Unexpectedly, the hobbits save Middle Earth. When Tolkien read Jesus' kingdom message he saw that God delighted to use little, unassuming people to transform the world. *You must become as a little child ...*

The kingdom will not advance through famous, rich, important people. It's going to advance by you humbling yourself to your friend, your neighbor, and your sphere of influence. It's going to advance by you reaching out and loving others, washing their feet, forgiving them, and not posturing behind false ego-props.

Jesus' approach changes everything and is contrary to our fallen nature. As individuals and congregations we need to take Jesus' approach seriously and quit trying to muscle mainstream culture in our direction. Contrary to Jesus' actions, we often believe we can out shout the world. The style of our approach is as much the message as the message itself. We must surrender and remain servants to find our wholeness through brokenness surrendered.

A few years ago a few hundred believers were gathered, praying on Mount Soledad. Our purpose was to protect the cross of Mount Soledad from cultural revisionists who want every religious symbol that stands on public property removed. The media was present and the evening moderator (and friend of mine), nicknamed "Bird," was trying to caution all the speakers and the people praying, "Please operate within the spirit of Jesus."

I knew what he was saying. *Please don't use the control-power paradigm to expand Jesus' kingdom. It's not becoming of the church.* But a couple of people did just that when they got to the microphone. "God, we pray that you judge those wicked people that want to tear down the cross. And we pray for these evil people to be exposed..." And I just thought: Oh, boy. We're all gracious, humble and forgiving until we don't get our way because we all think that our way is God's way.

Here's the stunning thing about Jesus. We expect the king to come through the front door and instead he slips in though the servant door on the side. Then he says, "Now you who follow me must operate in the kingdom paradigm: Blessed are the broken. The least shall be greatest. If you want to be great in the kingdom of God you must become the servant of all. Take up your cross and follow me."

CHILDREN, LAST AND LEAST

Jesus concludes in various Gospels by saying, *"Whoever finds his life will lose it. Whoever loses his life for my sake will find it."* In Luke 9:23 Jesus said, *"If anyone would come after me, he must deny himself, take up his cross daily and follow me."* In the next verse, he tells us, *"For whoever wants to save his life will lose it, but whoever loses his life for me will save it."* In Mark 9:35 he says, *"If anyone wants to be first, he must be the very last, and the servant of all."* In Mark 10:31, *"But many who are first will be last, and the last first."* And in Mark 10:15, *"I tell you the truth, anyone who will not receive the kingdom of God like a little child will never enter it."*

When my son, Jon, wrote the song, *Sooner or Later*, it had a profound effect on me. I was already a fan of the Danish philosopher, Soren Kierkegaard, but this song captured my heart and unveiled the Gospel as I had never seen it. In the chorus, Jon sings,

> Sooner or later they'll find there's a hole in the wall.
> Sooner or later you'll find out that you'll dream to
> be that small.

Then the song climaxes with,

> I gave it all away and lost who I am
> I threw it all away
> With everything to gain
> And I'm taking the leap
> With dreams of shrinking
> Yeah, dreams of shrinking[2]

Until this song I never associated the leap of faith and humility as being one and the same. I figured that humility would eventually come. *"I believe that Jesus died for my sins on the cross. And now that I'm a Christian, I'm going to start working on this humility thing."* Later I would become a child, become last and least. First I must become saved. I had never realized they were so connected, but to follow Wholly Jesus, we must abandon the power/control paradigm and become kings who serve. We let go of the giant sack of pride that keeps us from escaping through the tiny hole in the wall. We grab a hold of the humble savior: *we dream of shrinking*. There we will find ourselves becoming whole.

Many haven't made the seamless connection, as I hadn't. But humility is the nature of the kingdom. It is the tiny, little door to the giant castle. And we're already so big on our own. This is why it was so difficult for a rich ruler to get through the kingdom door. His ego and agenda didn't fit in the kingdom of God, like a camel didn't fit in the eye of a needle.

When Jesus washed his disciples' feet, he wasn't merely acting out his forthcoming death. He was acting out the nature of the invading kingdom. He was saying that God is going to be taking you through the small side door over and over again, not to advance your ego, but to advance his kingdom.

God is going to be using you to transform the world around you. But you're going to be used in a way that often goes unnoticed. And you're going to be tempted to say, "Oooh, they never thanked me" or "He didn't even notice what I did" or "She never even sent a card." But being a servant is a humble job—that is, if you look around to others for your motivation and praise.

Much like us, the disciples didn't get this initially. Right after Jesus washed their feet they said, "Lord, who's the greatest?" Can you imagine being Jesus and listening to the twelve stooges arguing over who is the greatest? They actually had a form of this argument three different times. One time one of their mother's went to Jesus and asked if her son could sit on his right or left hand? They thought that the way of the kingdom of God was just as it was in the world where power and control reigned. And each time Jesus said, *"That's the way it is in this world. But that's not the way it will be with me."*

So what is the application of this? If you go through the rest of Jesus' teaching you'll find out the application is simply this: Don't wear a God badge. Don't go around arresting people in the name of God and telling them they're wrong. Don't move your ego downfield at the expense of the kingdom. Instead, commit acts of kindness, sacrifice, humility and love; and commit them in secret. Later on we'll say, "Lord, when did we do these things?" He'll say, "When you fed the poor person, when you visited the prisoner, when you warmed the heart of the sick ... you were doing it to me and now I will reward you openly." He says when it comes to forgiveness, how often should we forgive someone? "If I forgive them seven times am I done?" "No, you forgive them seventy times seven."

Jesus brings the point home when he says, "If I as your master" the great one, the powerful one in this world, "have gone around as the underdog, the servant, so must you." Humility emerges out of wholeness. Servitude promotes wholeness. This is the nature of the new kingdom and you advance it even now by following me.

Do we not see this advancing today?

A New Paradigm

In the Hindu countries of India and Nepal, missionaries have for centuries operated with the trickle down theory for reaching the people with the gospel of Jesus. The reasoning was that an outcast or lower caste would follow a converted Brahmin, but never would a Brahmin follow a lower caste. For centuries the focus of the gospel has been on reaching the rich, the powerful and the very important people of India ... and without much success.

But now at the dawn of the 21st century things are changing. The kingdom is advancing as Jesus said it would. The caste system that has enslaved and subjected more human beings than any other philosophy on the planet is crumbling. There is a spiritual revival and a civil rights movement happening that dwarfs the Civil Rights movement of America and the Anti-apartheid movement of South Africa.

This amazing movement is a modern day expression of Jesus' kingdom. The last are becoming first, the least are becoming the greatest and the poor in spirit are beginning to rejoice.

Centers are being built in poor villages where the lower castes live. These centers offer education for children, medical treatment, vocation training, moral and spiritual training. The Dhalits are experiencing Jesus as more than simply a savior of their sins. They see him now as a humble crusader healing their lives in a wholly way. God is working from the bottom up. He is working with mangers, children and Dhalits. Down is up. The least are the greatest. The last shall be first. And wholeness is happening.

chapter eight

The Wholly Trojan Horse

That's when the irony hit me
That this was revenge
Love had descended
And stolen our pain
Away
— Jon Foreman

The story of the Battle of Troy has been passed down through history because of the Greeks' unique strategy used to win. There is no better way to describe Jesus' approach to wholeness and personal transformation than to equate it to the Trojan horse. He must get inside the walls of our kingdom to conquer us. We would do anything to win a partial form of wholeness, without having to let him inside. But Jesus is an invading king and he must get inside the city gates of our hearts to bring about wholeness.

But how will he get in? We all have guards posted at the gates. All our ammunition and armor is pointed at anyone coming through the front gate. We are armed with impressive arguments and justifications, we have stored up pain, confusion and bitterness, and we have seen the hypocrisy of religion. If he gets past our first defense, we have more arsenals to volley: "Who really wrote the Bible? What about the conflict between the Bible and science? What about the crusades and all the harmful things done in the name of Christianity?" As a last resort we dump all the junk over the wall—all that the church has done wrong: scandals of sex, abuse of money and the absurdness of certain "Christian" television shows. We are armed and ready for battle, and no one is getting in with these defenses we've prepared.

If God would stay outside the gates, a compromise would be possible. Jesus could be king of his realm and I of mine. God could heal my body, my marriage, my pocketbook, my business, and even remove my sins, but I would stay on the throne. Thankfully, Jesus still gets in ... and ultimately, we want him to be inside our gates.

***

Joshua is walking alone in the desert, miles from Jericho, the city he must conquer. He is alone, contemplating his strategy for victory, when suddenly he sees an armed warrior off in the distance. At first his image is blurred by the heat waves rippling off the desert floor, but as Joshua approaches he sees the warrior is alone with his scimitar drawn, prepared for battle and pointed directly at Joshua.

Joshua draws near to investigate, and he is prepared to accept the challenge. He inquires of the stranger, "Are you for us or for our enemies? Are you going to fight on our side or theirs? Are you going to do what we command or what they command? Are you taking orders from me, Joshua, or from their king?"

The warrior's answer pierces Joshua's soul. "Neither," he replied, "but as commander of the army of the LORD I have now come."

The discerning reader will know that the phrase *the army of the LORD* was a key phrase in Israel for the angelic army of God. Joshua was either standing in front of a powerful angel or this was an actual theophany (appearance of Yahweh). It was probably the latter because the warrior's first command to Joshua was to "Take off your sandals, for the place where you are standing is holy."

The simple truth of this divine moment is clear. We ask God, "Are you with us or not? Are you going to fit within our plans or not? Are you going to transform our lives they way we expect or not?" His answer is, "Neither. The real question is: Are you with me?"

King Jesus knows our will is the control room of our being. It is from this throne room that all our decisions come forth. Some decisions are amoral such as mere preferences of colors, music genres, vacation locations and friends. But some choices are seismic and ulti-mately affect our thinking, our bodies, our surroundings, our family and friends, and our world. It is this little thing called the will that is the tipping point of the two kingdoms. It was through the will that the Garden was surrendered. It is through our will that the king enters. And it is through our will that wholeness will come.

This is why Jesus commands that we surrender. We don't dip in here and there asking God to transform us on our terms. The heart of our transformation is in the willful act of surrender. All other transfor-mation follows that one act. Though this surrender is often recon-firmed, over and over again, it is our surrender that ignites and launches God's transformation in us and through us. It is our surren-der that opens the door to wholeness.

FOLLOWING JESUS TO THE CROSS AND BEYOND

The key to transformation is Jesus' absolute invasion. But once the content of the Trojan horse is released inside the walls of a heart, everything must change.

The pivotal event in our transformation was the cross and resur-rection. This was the Trojan Horse of God's kingdom. It is through this humanly unexpected event that Jesus conquered sin, death and all that is evil. Although the transformation of our lives and this world is far from complete, it is through faith in this event that transformation to wholeness in us and through us begins.

The first time Jesus used the term *cross* it was in the context of explaining the high cost of discipleship to his followers: *"If anyone would come after me, he must deny himself and take up his **cross** and fol-low me"* (Mark 8:34). Matthew's version is more exacting:

> Anyone who loves his father or mother more than me is not worthy of me; anyone who loves his son or daughter more than me is not worthy of me; and anyone who does not take his cross and follow me is not worthy of me. Whoever finds his life will lose it, and whoever loses his life for my sake will find it. (Matthew 10:37-39)

In these teachings the cross was a clear metaphor for cost and value. Jesus does not want a wishy-washy disciple who wants to barter. Jesus requires a certain response—an act of the will—a decision to die if necessary.

He repeated this again in a more dramatic context. He was telling the disciples that he must go to Jerusalem and suffer many things at the hands of the religious leaders and be killed to be raised to life. At this depressing sounding revelation Peter decided he would cheer Jesus up with some positive thinking, "Never, Lord. This shall never happen to you!"

Peter apparently was offended at the idea of the messiah dying. This was not in his theology, and he did not want this to happen to his friend and rabbi. But this was not how the story would end.

At this, Jesus rebuked Peter, calling him Satan. Then in this context he declares, *If anyone would come after me, he must deny himself and take up his cross and follow me.* For whoever wants to save his life will lose it, but whoever loses his life for me will find it (Matthew 16:24-25). Once again, Jesus opened the spreadsheet and asked his followers to balance the cost of following him. The expense of following Jesus, and thus finding wholeness, is losing our lives in every way imaginable. Modeling him is not enough. He is an invader, remember, and he will have all of you or none at all.

The surprising, all-or-nothing surrender will be unpleasant at times—this Jesus tells us—but any other path will not lead to wholeness. Jesus makes it clear that there is no alternative: "And anyone who does not carry his cross and follow me cannot be my disciple" (Luke 14:27). He cannot be whole.

***

Crucifixion was a Roman instrument of capital punishment that everyone knew. They had seen men who defied Rome hung on crosses to die. But Jesus' issue was with the religious leaders of Jerusalem, not Rome. Jesus predicted that he would be betrayed by a disciple and then condemned to death by the Sanhedrin (Mark 10:33), but the cross was a complete surprise to his followers. When he used the cross

KOORONG

Penrith

Tax Invoice (incl GST)

ABN # 93 001 583 759
www.koorong.com
Unit 3b, 61-79 Henry St, Penrith 2750
(02) 4724 4477

Till: 3
Operator: Jaker
Tran: 3064734   Cash   Sale
Date: 8/08/09   15:25

Item	Qty	Price	Disc %	Extn

Wholly Jesus
9780981770550   7.00   7.00

Total (incl GST of $ 0.64)   7.00
e Indicates price excludes GST

Tender Type		Amount

Cash   10.00

Tender Total   10.00
Change   3.00

Please retain for return or exchange

Thank you for shopping at

Koorong
Where Good Books Cost Less

as a metaphor for discipleship, his followers had no idea the metaphor would be Jesus' reality. And it is clear they did not understand the universal implications of his death and subsequent resurrection. Today, we don't have the luxury of being caught up in the moment. We must either surrender to the invasion that occurred or we must resist it. If we surrender to the invading king, the crucifixion and resurrection events are our bridge to wholeness.

Some modern theologians would like to make Jesus' death and resurrection an accident or a good run at messiah-ship gone bad. But in reality, Jesus intended to die. "Jesus resolutely set out for Jerusalem," writes Luke (9:51). Jesus knew that the events embodied God's Wholly Trojan Horse.

THE DECISIVE BLOW

The cross was a strategy that no one suspected—not even Satan. But it was the Wholly Trojan Horse that ultimately defeated the kingdom of darkness and re-paved the path to wholeness.

Still, I've found that most have not thought much about the cross. Many see it as a tragic ending to a beautiful life—like Romeo and Juliet, life ended unnecessarily. Others see the cross as a great act of love. Still others see Jesus like Socrates, loving truth more than life itself—a martyr for truth.

When the crowd yelled "CRUCIFY," they had no idea they were building the Trojan Horse. When Pilot washed his hands, he did not know he was opening the city gates to the Horse. When the Sanhedrin leveraged their influence against Jesus, they did not know they had made invasion possible. When the soldiers drove the nails into Jesus' hands and feet, no centurion suspected an invasion would be upon them in a matter of hours. When Jesus yelled the words, "It is finished!" no one realized it was only the beginning. When Jesus' body was laid in Joseph of Aremathea's tomb, no one suspected the Horse's belly would be rolled open and the Commander of a new kingdom would emerge with victory in his hands and on his breath.

Most believers simply see the crucifixion as the fulfillment of the Day of Atonement and our forgiveness of sins. And that it is. But it is much more than forgiveness and heaven. At the cross and resurrection, Jesus delivered his decisive blow to the kingdom of darkness and all its human allies. The world has never been the same.

The mutiny launched in the Garden of Eden was finally defeated. The chain reaction of brokenness was now itself broken. The kingdoms of bondage, sickness and death were defeated. Wholeness invaded. Bio-psycho-socio-spiritual redemption was offered to a broken world and those who accept it are free to be fully human again.

A passage that summarizes this great event is found in Isaiah 53:4-5:

> Surely he took up our infirmities and carried our
> sorrows, yet we considered him stricken by God,
> smitten by him, and afflicted. But he was pierced for
> our transgressions, he was crushed for our iniquities;
> the punishment that brought us peace was upon
> him, and by his wounds we are healed.

In these two events, humanity was invaded and ransomed. This "deeper magic" as C. S. Lewis called it, legally corrected and mystically accomplished all that was necessary to break the curse on this dark planet. It is more than expiation, more than propitiation, more than redemption, more than forgiveness. It is God's love breaking brokenness and announcing a wholly new day. Thus Jesus declares from his throne, "I am making everything new!" (Revelation 21:5).

It is no accident that even the weather and earth's crust itself reacted to Jesus' death. "From the sixth hour until the ninth hour darkness came over all the land" (Matthew 27:45).

> And when Jesus had cried out again in a loud voice,
> he gave up his spirit. At that moment the curtain of
> the temple was torn in two from top to bottom. The
> earth shook and the rocks split. The tombs broke
> open and the bodies of many holy people who had
> died were raised to life. They came out of the tombs,
> and after Jesus' resurrection they went into the holy
> city and appeared to many people (Matthew 27:50-
> 53).

The whole earth shook for joy the moment the curse was broken—even the dead were belched from their tombs. What a momentous picture of a whole new beginning.

When it comes to unpacking the breadth of salvation, many western theologians have focused on such things as who is and can be saved or on the order of salvation. Sadly, the daily application of salvation has been ignored.

The stoner, the person in marriage crises, the cripple, the clinically depressed and those rejected by society have not been told how Christ's full salvation applies to them as well as to anyone else. But the sanctification gap is as real as ever today. (Perhaps then it is not the theologians we should look to but the poets). My son Jon sings a song called "Revenge." It's sung by the thief on the cross, how Jesus had revenge on the world by allowing himself to be crucified. And in loosing he won, in dying he gave life, in his punishment he punished the world and had revenge—an ironic revenge of love. This was the trojan horse.

Furthermore, we interpret the cross and resurrection through our 2,000-year-old lenses. Because we rarely see bodies healed or characters transformed, we place all our weight on forgiveness and justification—two intangibles. We promise forgiveness and justification to all. But we promise sanctification much less often. We are not sure a person can be transformed in this life. We have lower expectations. But with our lower expectations, the power of the cross and resurrection becomes diluted. In contrast, the first disciples saw the power of the events firsthand and expected powerful transformation right then and there. Their expectations were high and their transformations were tangible.

This is why Paul could exclaim, "Therefore, if anyone is in Christ, he is a new creation; the old has gone, the new has come!" (2 Corinthians 5:17) It has come now.

STILL FEELING BROKEN

If Jesus laid such a significant blow to the kingdom of darkness and the kingdom of self, why then is this world, including me, so messed up? Why do people still die, why do we have wars, why do the poor suffer, why does it look like he never came? Why do children all over the world still go to bed hungry? Or their parents die of AIDS?

The problem of evil rears its ugly head. Some religions will tell us that brokenness is only an illusion. But an earthy faith like Judeo-Christianity is much too honest and cannot simply dismiss evil as an illusion. To paraphrase Lewis, we can't talk nonsense.[1]

Other religions take an extremely dualistic approach with two equal divine titans warring in the heavens (Zoroastrianism). But while there is a real devil in Christianity who leads this planet's mutiny, Jesus is on the throne. He is all-powerful, all-loving, omnipresent and fully just, yet evil still exits.

There is no doubt evil is an Achilles heel for the public relations of a good and sovereign God. But when free will, human responsibility, the devil, exponential brokenness, time, God's sovereignty and redeeming love are added to the mix, what precise percentage each plays in the structural equation of evil, I would be hesitant to say. Still, God's solution was the cross and resurrection. And on the last day we will know vastly more about God's grace than we can know now.

Our response must not be that of the child who got her hand caught in the cookie jar and asked, "Mommy, why did you allow the jar to be there to tempt me?" We must take responsibility if this world is ever going to change. God is a convenient scapegoat. To be sure, natural tragedies are very difficult to explain and I don't even try. I just weep with those who weep. But to blame God for the condition and exponentially broken choices seems a bit hard to swallow.

For the believer, the problem of evil is narrowed to be one of time. The question is not just, "Why does a good God allow bad things to happen?" It is rather, "Why does Jesus, who has defeated darkness, allow its effects to still linger? Why does he delay?" We live in this tension: the already-but-not-yet-world.[2]

We would prefer that the "already" part of the equation existed alone. We want everything put right now. Yet, we live in the tension of the in-between world. We see God's quick fix as an act of love, but often fail to see that his delay is also love: *The Lord is not slow in keeping his promise, as some understand slowness. He is patient with you, not want-*

ing anyone to perish, but everyone to come to repentance (2 Peter 3:9).

Rational answers can only go so far. Most questions about suffering are emotional. When I am with people who are suffering, there are no easy answers. I bury as many people as any pastor, complete with infant deaths, mothers who die young, and entire families who have died leaving one child behind. Pain is tragic pain, wrong is horrific wrong, and evil is maddening evil no matter how you slice it. I remember kicking beer cans and yelling at God in the alleys of Edinburgh because he had not visibly healed the needy people who came forward for prayer.

It would be wrong for me, in a moment of despair, to cut off the limb I am sitting on. Jesus has a wonderful track record of restoration and deserves no attacks from me. He died and rose to put things right. He laid his life on the line. He, too, wept at Lazarus' tomb. He is the "Lamb who rules and will be our shepherd, leading us to springs of living water and wiping away every tear from our eyes" (Revelation 7:17). I must see that he is clearly on my side.

To the believer, every disease is too long, every heartache is too great and every death is too soon. All die too young—even the aged. This planet and we humans are not created for pain and death, which is why they hurt so much. Death is an enemy, a mutation, that was dealt a final blow at the cross and resurrection, yet still gasps for air, still violently convulses and still does not surrender. The enemy of our souls is still alive, yet he knows he is defeated. Does not a defeated enemy, before his final breath, become more desperately violent?

Although the cross and resurrection were the climax of redemption, the enemy's surrender has not taken place. We are promised it will, but the kingdoms of this earth have yet to submit to the rightful king (Revelation 11:15). Brokenness still exists and must be resisted.

By God's design, the Wholly Trojan Horse event makes resistance possible. It provides a new default in our broken humanity. The default in our human system is presently set to "broken." Faith in Wholly Jesus' finished work resets the default to "whole." But it must be calibrated over and over or it will return to its old "broken" setting. Evil forces are like the counter-gravity that pulls our compass pin off true north. We speak of spiritual disciplines, which, in the kingdom mindset, means we must maintain our "whole" setting. We must resist the counter-gravity that pulls us back to the "broken" setting. As we resist the old, we begin to reflect, more and more of the image of God—we embody the image of our whole selves.

It is at times painfully clear we live in the "between" times—the "already-but-not-yet" era of history. It is here we can experience the "presence of the future."[3] We can celebrate Jesus' invasion and subsequent reign in our lives and his transforming work through us. *He who began a good work in us will complete it until the day of Christ Jesus.*[4]

Lewis put it this way: "Enemy-occupied territory—that is what this world is. Christianity is the story of the rightful king who has landed, you might say landed in disguise, and is calling us all to take part in a great campaign of sabotage. When you go to church you are really listening-in to the secret wireless from our friends…"[5]

Many have compared the cross and resurrection events to D-Day. As brutal as that day was, it was the day when the back of the enemy was broken. But two more years of war raged on until the Allied troops poured into Berlin. It is in a similar "between time" that we now live.

The enemy's back has been broken and the invading armies—the bearers of wholeness—are swelling to finalize the victory.

* * *

Troy was defeated the moment the great wooden horse was drawn inside the gates, though it would not have appeared that way to someone looking on. All appeared just as it had been moments before—as it had been for days, months and years before. But that night, the few brave troops hidden in the Horse's belly stepped out and opened the gates for their fellow warriors. A great battle ensued all night and into the next day. It was a battle destined for victory but one that still had to be fought. The enemy was defeated but would never lie down without a fierce, bloody fight. We now battle in much the same way—we battle for a new kingdom and for the broken people of this world who do not yet know what is coming.

TRANSFORMATION FOR YOU AND THE WORLD

It is unfair and perhaps unwise to only talk mystically and spiritually about transformation without becoming concrete. We must ask: How does a person actually change, not simply in a veneer way but really become a new person? How does a person appropriate the cross and resurrection in real life? Can a person truly be physically or mentally healed? Does it happen all the time? How does culture, society and the world transform to wholeness? Does it all wait for the second coming or does it truly enter into time and space now? The remainder of this book will attempt to answer these questions. They are the questions Christians have been asking for centuries but have perhaps failed or forgotten to ask through the lens of our Wholly King Jesus.

Wholly Jesus is always on the side of life, wholeness and justice. There is no dualism whereby we must wait and see if God is good or bad today, to find out what side of the bed he woke up on. He has committed himself to the side of good and displayed it on the cross.

But God is a God of many means. He uses all kinds of people, events, times and healing agents to accomplish his transforming will. It is therefore nonsense to speak of medicine or therapy as second best to supernatural healing. God sometimes heals supernaturally, sometimes through prayers, and sometimes through oil or medicine. God uses many things to perpetually move us closer to wholeness. To be sure, there are side effects with some remedies and not others, and some therapists are better than others, but God welcomes any practitioner who wants to work with him, even if our tools are inferior to his.

It is clear that we are not to obsess over our own transformation—if we obsess about anything, it should be the transformation of others around and through us. *Seek first the kingdom of God and all these things will be added to your life.* It is Jesus we seek and his invading kingship to which we surrender. We must see that our wholeness is ultimately an *alien wholeness*—we only become whole through an outside force invading us, not by a means present in ourselves. To pursue wholeness without pursuing Jesus is to repeat the crime of the Garden all over again. All wholeness has Jesus at its center, so it makes sense that the focus of the New Testament is to reconcile people to him, not to a therapeutic agenda. He is the power behind wholeness.

Jesus is the standard and wholeness is the direction of the kingdom. We must actively maintain alignment with both. The message of Wholly Jesus is that it takes an invasion of the soul, mind and body to bring about a holism that is more profound than any offering today.

The message longs to give birth to messengers—our lives must become the message. Belief in Jesus, his death and resurrection is key to our salvation. Then our lives join the message by becoming the message of transformation. Without Christians, wholeness is only a future hope. With Christians, wholeness can be now.

STORIES OF SACRIFICE FOR WHOLENESS

Perhaps the most amazing part of the kingdom message is what is implied and not said: That God, through Jesus, wants us. He wants us back. He wants to redeem us to wholeness and therefore he must love us.

Some get it and some don't. Tonight I sat around a bonfire on the beach of Chacala, Mexico, listening to 40 pastors and their spouses tell their commitment to wholeness. They were tales of how far and at what cost they had traveled to come to a very simple leadership conference. Some had traveled three days by car, some by bus, and one couple had hitchhiked 15 hours with their precious daughter who had Down syndrome, to arrive at the simple gathering. Most are village pastors who support themselves by other means and a few are urban pastors. These beautiful people talked into the night under the brilliant stars and bobbing mast lights of sailboats anchored in the cove.

I can't remember the last time I heard a story of great sacrifice in the U.S. I have heard such stories in Egypt, Algeria, Mauritania, Sudan, Moldova, Nepal, Bhutan and Cambodia. I know pastors who traveled for days on foot through the Himalayan foothills to hear teaching from a California pastor. These stories ultimately express the great value people around the world place on the wholeness Jesus offers.

PART III:

HOW HALF PEOPLE
BECOME WHOLE

chapter nine

Raising the Bar to Normal

*We shall bleed and squeal as the handfuls of fur come out; and then,
surprisingly, we shall find underneath it all a thing we have never
yet imagined: a real Man, an ageless god, a son of God, strong,
radiant, wise, beautiful, and drenched in joy.*

— C.S. Lewis

S he was doing all the talking while he sat as stiffly guarded as a statue. She wanted their marriage to work. He didn't care. She was transparent about her own faults and his. He was only grunting when he agreed and rolling his eyes when he didn't.

They called themselves Christians, but I wasn't sure how much of their faith was merely a label. I knew they attended church. But an old southern saying danced in my head, "Just 'cause you're born in a oven, it don't make you a biscuit." How much had they actually allowed Jesus to invade their lives?

I asked the husband to tell me about his spiritual journey. And as I suspected, there wasn't much to tell. Being a Christian was about going to church when he felt like it. Otherwise there was no connection between his daily life and his faith.

I was getting nowhere fast. Every open-ended question met a brick wall. Finally, I asked him point blank if Jesus was his Lord. He said, "Of course, what else would he be?" ... "Is he your master?" I responded. "What do you mean?" he asked. Then with a flash of insight I asked, "Is he your boss?"

Immediately there was a tightening of his eyes. "If you're asking me if I let Jesus boss me around and tell me what to do, you have another thing coming. I decide what I do, where I go, what I say and who I am. I go to church and that's enough. And that's just the way it is."

I was thrilled and laughed. "Bingo," I said. We finally had traction, contact.

I don't think this man's religion is unusual. It is fairly normal. Many believers don't see Jesus as the invading, transforming king, but as the acquiescent savior who awaits our arrival in heaven. He has forgiven us and now awaits us. These two bookends of the faith are intact: forgiveness and heaven. But many believers buy into the notion that how we live between the bookends is up to us. We are bookend-Christians, ignoring the volumes of potential transformation in between, and assuming we've got it all.

But when this form of Christianity is held against Scripture, it is the aberration not the rule. The norm for centuries has been to see character change as the most important part of our salvation. Forgiveness gets us into the presence of Wholly Jesus where sanctification then begins—sanctification that is at its core, without a doubt, movement toward wholeness. For a person to follow Jesus without a constantly transforming character is subnormal. The bar needs to be raised to normal.

TRANSFORMATION OF CHARACTER—AN ANCIENT LONGING AND EXPECTATION

Many ancient religions and societies have held up good character as the jewel of their culture. In Asia, Hinduism, Buddhism, Confucianism and Taoism, all place heavy emphasis on the formation of character and moral behavior. Islam, as controversial as extremists have made the religion, has a strong emphasis on ethics. Even the lesser-known religions of Shintoism and Animism have important moral behavioral expectations. Judaism, too, has one of the most exhaustive lists of character and moral expectations of any religion. It was the centerpiece of Greek philosophy. C. S. Lewis built an entire book, *Abolition of Man*, on the principle of the Tao—universal moral character. It's apparent that all religions around the world agree on a basic code of behavior.[1]

But when it comes to the subject of wholeness, the unique element that Jesus brings to the discussion is that of transformation into the image of God. Our character is not simply formed through knowledge, rituals and discipline. One is transformed by faith in the work and power of Wholly Jesus.

The Imago Dei is the Holy Grail for humanity. It is what we are in search of constantly. It is how we live in the painting of life. We were meant to possess the character of God. Jesus came to bring us not only to God through forgiveness, but also to transform us into God's image, returning us to the blueprint of God's original design, returning us to fully human. Without this process, we are merely beings who are *almost* human.

Unfortunately in Western Christianity, transformation has played second fiddle to forgiveness for much of the last century. It's time to become truly human and truly whole.

Jesus in the Sermon on the Mount

Jesus in the Sermon on the Mount raised the bar of Judaism from merely good, veneer behavior, or "sin management," to loving intent integrated with authentic behavior. Many believers teach and act as if Jesus doesn't care much about our behavior because he "delivered us from the law." They think he only cares about the unseen heart. But nothing could be further than the truth. We have earlier made the case that this mistaken thinking comes from Docetic Gnosticism, not Christianity. Jesus himself said this in Matthew 5:17-20:

> Don't think that I have come to abolish the law or the Prophets: I have not come to abolish them but to fulfill them. I tell you the truth, until heaven and earth disappear, not the smallest letter, not the least stroke of a pen, will by any means disappear from the Law until everything is accomplished. Anyone who breaks one of the least of these commandments and teaches others to do the same will be called least in

the kingdom of heaven, but whoever practices and teaches these commands will be called great in the kingdom of heaven. For I tell you that unless your righteousness surpasses that of the Pharisees and the teachers of the law, you will certainly not enter the kingdom of heaven.

He did not come to erase moral or ethical expectations, but instead to actually fulfill them in his life and death, then to transform us to live increasingly within the law of the kingdom—the law of love.

In the Sermon, he says it's not enough to keep an oath, avoid adultery, abstain from murder or remain fair to others and love your neighbor. These moral laws are common throughout the world and don't get to the heart of the matter. Jesus raises the standard to integrated transformation by telling people to stop hating and always forgive. Don't lust, he says, or force your spouse to remarry by abandoning them. Be of such strong character that you don't even need to make a promise. Don't just be fair; be kind and giving. Don't just love your neighbor; love your enemies and pray for them. This, he says, is the essence of the transformation to wholeness that will take place in those who follow me.

He sums up his expectations for kingdom citizens by saying, "Be perfect like your heavenly Father." This is not perfectionism, as it is unhealthily modeled by rigid personalities. Rather, this is an invitation to become complete, integrated, whole. It is an invitation to leave the sub-human existence for a full humanity.

The entire teaching of the Sermon follows the purpose statement Jesus gave his followers in the beginning—*to be salt and light*. This means that the believers' lives are to be so different and transformed that they do good works (salt and light). This causes everyone to know that their transformation comes from God. If we are transformed people, Jesus says, we will be recognized as the offspring of our Father—possessing the characteristics of his image.

The command to be salt and light is no different than the first mandate to be God's image on earth. God's plan is firm and he will have his way: a world that sees the wonderful nature of an invisible

God through his earthly, human children, and in turn is drawn to him in worship and love. Jesus seamlessly ties personal transformation to outward transformation. This should be no surprise in a holistic, integrated world. When we are transformed, the world around us is transformed.

THE CAUSE AND EFFECT OF TRANSFORMATION

Everyone understands the concept of cause and effect. If I eat, drink or use a commercial product, I want to know: what's the outcome? Many products are sold by convincing the buyer of some extraordinary change that will come into a person's life. We see the before and after pictures in their advertisements. We will be more attractive, richer, stronger, and healthier if we drink, eat or use this product. It's cause and effect and it's natural to our thinking. We live in a cause and effect world.

The same is true of Wholly Jesus. Our friends want to know what happens to a person who "drinks" our product. What's the effect of Wholly Jesus? Will they become weird, self-righteous, or preachy if they become a Christian? People really are watching and want to know what will happen to a follower.

Some have tapped into this concept to build their own wealth. They preach that a person will become rich and healthy if he or she believes and follows Jesus. There is a grain of truth to this if they mean that God will provide for us and he wants to bring wholeness into our lives, and that the process will not be complete until we are in his presence. However, usually that is not what is meant, and the fine print of pain, loss and brokenness in this life is left off the label. Everything is presented in simple, black-and-white terms to make "the sale." Once the listener donates healthily to the ministry, the preacher becomes wealthier. This is the health-and-wealth gospel.

The selling point of Christianity is not cosmetic wealth and health; it is transformed lives at the core of our character. Michael Green, in his book *Evangelism in the Early Church*, makes a strong argument for the case that transformed lives were once the primary preaching tool.[2] The character of Christians was a megaphone of truth

to their neighbors. It is what turned the Roman world upside down.
It is what is penetrating restricted countries today where believers are
disallowed to publicly speak of Wholly Jesus. Transformed lives were
once the salt and light of the world that could not be hidden or
silenced.

But this has not been the emphasis in the west. We have bumper
stickers that say "Christians aren't perfect, just forgiven" to eliminate
any expectation by observers to see any positive effect in our lives—to
eliminate the accountability of observation. Some have even marginalized the Sermon on the Mount by saying that it applies to us only
after the second coming of Christ. The church as a whole has made
transformation a stepchild or an addendum to the primary message of
forgiveness. Originally, they were twins and went hand in hand, just
like the cross and resurrection.

The question we must ask again, as if for the first time is this: If
Wholly Jesus was in a bottle and we drank every last drop, what would
be the effect? What would we feel, think, do? How would we change?
What would our friends and neighbors begin to notice? What would
it be? What would be the effect of a whole bottle of Jesus?

GOD'S DESIGN—LOVE FOR LOVE

Scripture is rich with passages about the transformed life. There
are so many it is impossible to ignore. The second half of most of
Paul's letters deals specifically with the effects of transformation.
Perhaps the most well known passage is Romans 12:1-2. Here, Paul
gives us one of the clearest pictures of transformation:

> Therefore, I urge you, brothers, in view of God's
> mercy, to offer your bodies as living sacrifices, holy
> and pleasing to God—this is your spiritual act of
> worship. Do not conform any longer to the pattern
> of this world, but **be transformed** by the renewing
> of your mind. Then you will be able to test and
> approve what God's will is—his good, pleasing and
> perfect will.

Paul does not gently coax his readers but urges them to the transformed life. The word means *to plead, entreat, exhort, beseech*. Transformation is no suggestion. It is what Paul points to throughout the entire letter of Romans.

The simple cause Paul gives for transformation is God's love. Paul has been speaking of the love of God all along. Chapter eight, which is a prelude to Chapter 12, ends in a crescendo regarding God's love:

> No, in all these things we are more than conquerors through him **who loved us**. For I am convinced that neither death nor life, neither angels nor demons, neither the present nor the future, nor any powers, neither height nor depth, nor anything else in all creation, will be able to separate us from **the love of God** that is in Christ Jesus our Lord.

There is no question from any portion of the New Testament that God is a God of love and it is his redeeming love that has orchestrated the cross and resurrection events to provoke a response.

Objectively we see God's love primarily at the cross. Certainly creation was an act of love, God's unseen grace in leading us to himself was love, and his ongoing guidance and provision comes from his love. But we know his love primarily and unequivocally from the historical event of Calvary. *For God loved the world in this way: he gave his only unique son.*

Our pursuit of transformation and the transformation of this world can never take place apart from his love. It must be the beacon always held in view for us to see. It was God's move toward us and it must be ours toward God. Christianity is a love religion—love is the cause, love is the effect. Love is what transforms us and love is the result of transformation.

Sailors are always attentive to landmarks when sailing into a harbor. There is usually a buoy, a lighthouse or a marker that allows the sailor to align his sight. Without the objective markers, the sailor must trust his subjective instincts. Far too many a sailor has run aground or sunk in this manner.

Far too many believers trust their subjective feelings when it comes to their faith. Yet, it is God's objective love with which we must align ourselves. With God's love in sight as a marker in the harbor, now it's our turn to respond to his sacrificial love.

THE NECESSARY EFFECT

Now we are urged to *offer* ourselves to God in love. The language Paul uses in Romans is that of the Jewish sacrificial system. The sacrificial system is fulfilled in Christ. He is the Lamb of God who takes away the sins of the world. But sacrifices continue in a new and living way. We sacrifice ourselves, in love and devotion to him. No longer do we use an animal or grain on an altar. We offer ourselves. We are living, breathing human sacrifices.

For the effect to come to fruition, it is our bodies (*soma*) that we must offer. In the Western world, we expect to offer our souls or hearts. But Paul specifically mentions bodies to make a point. It is through our bodies that the decisions of life are acted out. Our eyes, our tongues, our hands, our feet and our minds carry out the physical expression of our hearts.

We are to *somatize* rather than spiritualize the Gospel. Christianity is an incarnate religion. We are an outward expression of an inward work. It's cause and effect all over again. We work out our salvation, because it is God who is at work in us (Philippians 2:12-13). So it is our bodies that are offered, just as Jesus offered his body for us. Only we remain alive—living sacrifices.

In other letters Paul uses different language. Instead of the sacrificial phrase *to offer*, he uses two other metaphors: one of changing clothes and the other of execution. We are to take *off* the old, dirty clothing, and *put on* the new godly apparel (Ephesians 4:22; Colossians 3:12). We are also to *execute* our old sinful nature that wants to resurrect itself and live again (Colossians 3:5). We are to redecide that our old nature has already died with Christ and our new nature already lives in him (Colossians 3:3). It is in the act of surrender that transformation is ignited. Active trust is the catalyst that promotes God's invasion within. The offering of the territory of my being to his Lordship expands the Kingdom of God within. In that act my crown of dominion is laid at his feet.

It is this act of offering that is *holy and pleasing to God, our spiritual or logical act of worship* (Romans 12:1). So much is made of worship services today. Worship has, in fact, become an industry. That's fine, but an hour's worship service is a hair's breath of our entire lives which are called to be sacrifices. The offering of our physical lives is a never-ending worship service that speaks volumes louder than anything we do on Sunday.

We have a cunning way of divorcing our religious life from our daily, material world. But it is in the physical world that our spirituality is ultimately measured. The rest is just talk, theory, emotional music and good intentions. A person's ultimate concern is found where he or she spends their time, energy and money through the use of their body. What we offer the parts of our physical beings to is, in fact, what we worship. So as we sacrifice our bodies to God, we are worshipping. The effect is always evident and tangible—not merely felt.

Paul knew where the cause and effect transformation often gets hung up. This is why he said, *no longer be conformed to the patterns of the world … (Romans 12:2)*. The pattern of this world is the prevailing value system and corresponding behavior of our existing culture. Remember that we are by nature imitators, mirrors, images of something or someone else. If we are to be transformed, we must stop mimicking the patterns of this mutinous world and instead mimic the *patterns* of Wholly Jesus.

The ultimate effect is change into his image—the image of God. We, in turn, reflect God's nature to others, thus bringing transformation to our sphere of influence. And this happens in *an ever-increasing way … from glory into glory* (2 Corinthians 3:18).

The New Testament is replete with encouragements, exhortations and commands to allow our belief to change our thinking and behavior. Almost every epistle has a transformation section that deals with expected changed behavior. Our faith in the cross and resurrection is to bring us into both forgiveness and transformation. The end result is that we become the salt of the earth, the light of the world, and the image of God on earth. We are meant to be an image of wholeness for those who are broken; and when we are, Wholly Jesus' offering is difficult to dispute. If the effect of Wholly Jesus' transformation to wholeness were global, it would be impossible to ignore.

FAULTY OR PARTIAL SOLUTIONS

So how has the modern church dealt with the subject of transformation?

Overall, not well. There have been many partial or faulty solutions. We mean well but we often approach the issue with half-hearted attempts that do not succeed. Many Western believers have never heard a compelling, integrated presentation of transformation. We thus have allowed many short-changed notions to rule. To take hold of the wholly transformation that God intends for us—and intends to use through us—we must first rid ourselves of the obstacles to the whole transformation Wholly Jesus offers.

1. The Intention of Good. This is goodness for goodness sake, not Christian transformation. It is sin management, as opposed to whole surrender and sacrifice. True Christianity only knows love and goodness that comes from obedience to Jesus. While we all want to be good, and we value goodness, Christians must know that it is fruitless to try to be good without Jesus' invading will. It is in the ingestion of the King's will by trust and surrender that I am changed.

Attempts to be good for goodness' sake work for easy behavioral changes, but they don't reach to the core of our problems. Jesus said that it was out of the heart that evil things come. We must be changed at the core of our being or we only whitewash the house and leave the termites to continue their destruction.

2. Automatism. Automatism, a term borrowed from Simon Chan, is one the most common myths in Western Christianity.[3] It is an unspoken heresy built on the misunderstanding of grace. It is the belief that if I sit passively in church, read my Bible for 10 minutes a day and pray at meals, Jesus will automatically change me. "It's his move, not mine. I want to change, but I can't until he changes me. Anything beyond this is my effort, which is work and violates Paul's teaching on grace. I do nothing; Christ does everything."

This thinking takes a strong and good belief in grace and misinterprets it to imply passivity. It is true that Jesus said, "*Without me you can do nothing*" *(John 15:5)*. We are dependent on God for everything. But Jesus also said in the same passage, *If you abide in me and I in you, you will bear fruit.. . . if you obey my commands you will abide . . . my command is this: that you love each other as I have loved you.* Responsive obedience, "Yes Lord," is a part of the transformational life. If a man remains in me and I in him, he will bear much fruit. We are called to "work out" the wholeness Jesus has worked into us (Philippians 2:12-13). We work it out (we shine as light and salt) and we take it (our will) seriously because it's God (God's will) who is volcanically stirring us to do so.

We are to respond to God's grace, and he has given us the ability to do so. We are response-able. We do not minimize God's grace by emphasizing our response, but maximize the effect of grace. The command to be transformed in Romans 12:2 is not addressed to God, it is written to us. *We* are to offer ourselves; *we* are to not conform; *we* are to be transformed by the renewing of our mind. In other words, we are to respond to God's grace and by his grace become salt and light for this world.

A command involves a response of the will: a yes or a no—activity, not passivity. Yes, God has given us a new heart but the heart must cooperate tangibly. Automatism is a fantasy that has paralyzed the church. True grace does not promote passivity but responsibility. This new life makes us *response-able*.

3. Eventism is the belief that I can be transformed in a moment by engaging in one more event: a conference, a special service, or through someone laying hands on me in prayer. We are, if we are honest, event-oholics. We travel to conferences, festivals and meetings searching for a moment that will transform us without pain or the exercise of our wills. We lay hands on each other praying that in a moment God will change a person's character. But eventism borders on magic.

It is not that I am against conferences or Christian events or the laying on of hands in prayer. I practice all of these myself. But it is the "in-place of" mentality that is wrong. It is wishful, pixie-dust thinking.

These things can't replace old-fashioned obedience. The hard "Yes, Jesus" must be learned and spoken. There is not an event on earth that can make you or me kind and loving. Transformation comes through obediently responding to the grace of God. Just as a butterfly develops its ability to fly through its struggle to climb out of the cocoon, so the believer's character is transformed in the tough moments of obedience.

4. Charismatic leader. We often search for someone who will transform us by laying his hands on us, speaking over us or deciding for us. I believe in the charismata. And I believe in dynamic leadership. But no leader's voice or limbs can change my character.

There used to be a commercial about banking, where a dignified old banker ended the spot by saying, "We do it the old fashion way; we earn it." Well, we certainly don't and never will earn anything, but the old fashion way of character transformation is by a visceral response of obedience. It must come from me. It was by the will of the first couple that the world was lost, and it is by our redeemed will that transformation occurs in us and through us.

Obedience has somehow become the nasty "O" word in the Christian world. We seem to avoid speaking it because, deep down, we want things changed quickly. But the old hymn is as true now as it ever was: "Trust and obey for there is no other way..."

5. Bibliolatry. We think that if we read enough we will automatically change. Reading the Bible is only one-third of the equation. I must respond to what I read in the power of the Spirit. It is wonderful to read the Bible daily but not because it is magic. God's word primes the pump that enables me to see him, myself, others and life from his perspective—from truth. But I must respond to the truth so it will take hold in my life.

Without a response, reading alone can even inoculate me to what God really wants to do. It can become a "check the box" exercise that's not connected with my character at all. The goal is not to read the Bible through as many times as possible in a lifetime. Rather, the goal is to see God glorified throughout the earth by transformed people transforming the world.

Jesus said that his followers were to be doers of the word, not listeners only. We have become a generation of listeners, readers, students, teachers and expositors; but are we also doers? Without doing, we are know-it-all houses built on the sand.

6. Truce with sinful self. We give up and decide that we can't change beyond this point. In our transformation we hit a tough part of our character or behavior that doesn't budge. We simply decide to stop growing and pitch our tent at some plateau. It feels too hard and there are too many failures.

This is precisely the area in which we need to be vigilant. Jesus was clear, *if your right hand offends you, cut it off. If your eye offends you gouge it out (Matthew 5:29-30)*. Thankfully we are not to take this literally or we would all be Cyclops with missing limbs. But the hyperbole is clear; we must be vigilant to conquer the resistant rebels within our being.

We must at the same time disallow truces with the sinful self, especially the typical "churchie" kind of sins: gossip, self-righteousness, slander, abuse of power, greed, manipulating others through fear, guilt or God-language. All these sins, when they are a lifestyle, are truces we have made with the old self, snatching our crowns back and seeking to co-rule the kingdom with Jesus.

7. Performance religion. We decide that through following rules we can change. Rules are good for easy behavioral transformation: what to wear, when to talk, what words to use. This is not transformation, merely behavioral adaptation.

Cognitive-behavioral psychology has had some amazing successes in dealing with such conditions as phobias, anxieties and even depression. As wonderful as that is, it is not necessarily spiritual transformation.

Religion, too, can fall short of transformation and be guilty of negative behavioral adaptation. This occurs when the convert learns the right language and behavior to fit in with the crowd and avoids the negative consequences. This occurs often in cults and marginal churches but it also occurs far too often in extreme fundamentalism. The slogan is, "Come in and receive the love of God, and if you don't do things our way, we will judge and slander you in the name of God to protect the church." Positive and negative behavioral adaptation to reach positive or avoid negative consequences is not the transformation of a person. It is how we train our pets.

The picture of Jesus transforming the woman caught in adultery or the woman at the well clearly depicts God's approach. In both cases, Jesus delivered the woman from an approach to God that was based on rigid rule keeping, and brought each one into true forgiveness and transformation.

8. Propositionalism. We are only propositionally changed, but not in reality.

With this unspoken belief, many in the church will say we are transformed by faith in Christ (in theory) but that it is impossible to change much in reality in this life. This is the typical strong-in-theology/weak-in-practice problem in the church.

This is theological mumbo jumbo. If we are propositionally transformed, there is an effect in real time and space. There may be areas in our lives that we wait for "by faith" but it is far more than a proposition. Faith is not a cop-out but a firm Biblical hope. Justification is not a substitute for sanctification.

Of course we walk by faith. But we can't be presumptuous and "claim" things are transformed that aren't. Of course we wait for Christ's return. But the kingdom has broken into this present darkness and is working in small and great ways. That is our expectation. The yeast may be invisible now but it is there working through the entire batch of dough. Transformation is happening inside and out, upward and outward.

9. Self-improvement. We personify *The Little Engine That Could*. We try harder, read more, do everything more. So we insatiably buy books and magazines, take vitamins and herbs, and seek therapists and gurus who will guide us to wholeness. This is the hottest Western approach at this time. The flaw here is that there is no compass or guiding map. The *Imago Dei* is missing. And the trust is in us rather than in Wholly Jesus. Our trust must be in the one we reflect and our power comes from him.

10. Focus on internal or external transformation to the neglect of the other. This has been quite typical of our binary world. We can't seem to pat our heads and rub our stomachs at the same time. We want to be introspective and fix ourselves or we forget about being transformed and attempt to transform the world. Both are seamlessly part of the kingdom of God. Transformation is God's work in and through us without separation. It is not an either/or proposition but a both/and process.

The life of God (*Imago Dei*) calls us to give ourselves away to others. That is the abundant life. The God-life is giving ourselves to others in love. It is more blessed. God gave himself to us at creation, in the incarnation, at the crucifixion and in giving us the Spirit. Self-giving is the image of God. It is the fully human life.

It is nonsense, except when speaking to co-dependent rescuers, to say "you must first love yourself before you can love others." Loving ourselves involves loving others. There is no chronology. They are seamlessly tied together. Our wholeness is tied to learning to give ourselves away. The more whole we become, the more we sacrifice for others.

11. Viewing transformation as simply going from bad to good. Changed lives are more than just going from bad to good. Some of our decisions and loving behavior must go from good to better to best. If we only are concerned with eliminating bad behavior, our transformation will be minimal. God wants our love for others to grow in insight and wisdom so that we can discern what is best (Philippians 1:9-10). Sometimes the enemy of the best is not the bad but the good. As we walk with Jesus he will teach us what is best in our love for others.

12. "Who cares? I'm going surfing!" Many times I have wanted to take this stance, and perhaps from time to time I have. "The world's problems and mine seem so complicated; why try? It's God's sovereign problem. Whatever. Let's just do what we like to do and not think about it."

Denial is a common reaction to most troubles. Denial can be corporate as well as individual. Like ostriches, we can stick our heads in the sand and hope the problem goes away.

I remember teaching one of my first sermons as a youth pastor in a Presbyterian church. One of the youth who happened to be fully deaf developed a bad case of hiccups. His hiccups were so loud during my message that his body would actually hop every 30 seconds. The church sat still, as if this wasn't happening. No one offered a glass of water; no one even suggested any of the many possible solutions. Everyone sat stone-faced, facing forward like good obedient children. And I was the worst. I kept preaching. This is abnormal! Normal is to stop and help.

Transformation, the restoration of the Imago Dei, is the jewel of salvation. Nothing could be more wonderful than millions of faces looking increasingly like Jesus. Therefore, the church must become as familiar with the truth of sanctification as we are with forgiveness and justification. How much can a person become like God in this life? No one knows the answer, but partial and faulty solutions won't help. There is no expectation from me of sinless perfection in this life. But we must expectantly give ourselves to a life of loving others as Christ has loved us.

As congregants come to pastors with the hope of truly changing we must be willing to handle the messy stuff such as addiction, mental health, family abuse, financial debt and marital and family dysfunction. But that just defensively gets us to the fifty-yard line.

We must equally be proactive, teaching and offering practical ways to display Christ's love in our spheres of influence: school, neighborhoods, work, family and recreation. We should encourage churches that are pioneering ways to help others in this way and be slow to criticize. The church must be known as the safest place on earth, where we can come with problems, and also be the most practical place to discover and practice the love of Christ. It should be known as the loving face of Christ on earth.

The cornerstone to Christ-centered transformation is ongoing faith in Jesus' power and his finished work on the cross. Our new character is not discovered through introspection, but as I love and serve Jesus and others. Transformation is experienced as an ongoing worship service whereby I offer or surrender myself to him throughout the day. It is a process, happening in key moments, throughout a lifetime.

TAKING WHOLLY JESUS SERIOUSLY ... AND RAISING THE BAR

When most people signed up to follow Jesus, it was the most exciting day of their lives. The adventure had begun. What could this mean, to be right with God and finally whole?

It's easy to become numb to this new life. There is a tendency, intrapersonally and interpersonally, to return to a previous state. The stretched spring too easily returns to its resting place. We see our sameness and the unchanged lives of others, so we stop expecting change at all. The adventure is over before it really began.

Recently my wife and I were on vacation in Hawaii and a couple on the beach recognized us from home and said hello. They, too, were on vacation. We had two wonderful days of getting acquainted. While walking with our snorkel gear to a spot called Tunnels on the north shore of Kauai, I asked my new friend to tell me his spiritual journey. He eagerly told me that five years ago at our church he decided to begin following Jesus and his wife made the same decision at the same time. Then he said, "Since then our life has been changed, and all our friends and relatives have noticed the drastic transformation."

I immediately thought of what Jesus said, *"You are the light of the world ... let your light shine before men, that they may see your good deeds and praise your Father in heaven."* I was beaming with delight. It was music to my ears. It was "normal." It was as it should be.

This normal of which I speak is to be radically, consistently and threateningly transformed by the love and power of Jesus. This is the bar to which we must raise our expectations in the Western church.

Jonathan Edwards was once challenged by the old guard of the Congregational church (the Old Lights) to give a response for the unseemly outbursts among converts (New Lights) that were occurring during the reading of his sermons. This was an extension of the ongoing debate between those Calvinists who emphasized God's election, and those Calvinistic evangelicals who insisted on a conversion experience. His retort was that the Old Lights owed him an explanation as to how they could be in the presence of a living God and not have some radical experience. It is, I believe, the better question. In the presence of Wholly Jesus, transformation is a forgone conclusion.

chapter ten

Becoming Spirit People

Jesus said, "Peace be with you! As the Father has sent me, I am sending you." And with that he breathed on them and said, "Receive the Holy Spirit."

— John, the Beloved

The wind had significantly picked up and I had to reduce the size of my sail. Lake windsurfing is sketchy; these overpowering gusts can blow hard then stop at anytime. Still, there is nothing like the feeling and anticipation of the wind on my back as I lean out over the water. Nothing is holding me up but a force I can't see; nothing giving lift to my sail but the invisible.

Once on shore, I spotted a couple I knew and struck up a conversation. Both wanted to try their hand on a board. After some quick instructions, I just let them go for it. Kelly picked it up better than Tom, and toward the end of the afternoon she had made it to the middle of the lake. I was a bit concerned because it was getting sultry and the wind was fading. Then what I feared would happen, happened. The air went still. Kelly dropped the sail into the water and looked helplessly to shore.

I did the only thing I knew: I dove into the water and swam to her. Only once I reached her, I realized I didn't have a plan. I knew she couldn't swim that far back to shore, so I decided to try something different. I put Kelly at the front of the board on her knees, and I hoisted the sail out of the water. Then I tried to create my own wind by pulling sharply on the boom. For a brief moment I could fill the sail with a false wind that pushed the board forward just a bit. Occasionally there was a little breeze to help, but progress was very slow. Finally, I had to rest the boom on the back of the board and paddle both of us to shore. Windsurfers weren't made for paddling. Neither were our lives.

We are made for the wind of the Wholly Spirit of Jesus to fill our beings. We are made to feel God's wind at our back—to have him influence, motivate, equip, empower and transform us. We are Spirit-beings and without the Wholly Spirit, we either become immobilized or overexerted.

This is what Jesus said to a religious teacher who secretly came to him:

> "I tell you the truth, no one can enter the kingdom of God unless he is born of water and the Spirit. Flesh gives birth to flesh, but the Spirit gives birth to spirit. You should not be surprised at my saying, 'You must be born again.' The wind blows wherever it pleases. You hear its sound, but you cannot tell where it comes from or where it is going. So it is with everyone born of the Spirit" (John 3:5-8).

No emphasis on the work of Jesus' Spirit could be strong enough. We are far more dependent on him than we often realize. Without the Spirit, we are but windsurfers stuck in the middle of a still lake. Our beings are made to be guided by the Wholly Spirit. Where the Spirit goes, we go, but only if we allow our sails to be filled.

Ultimately, this is the forward motion of transformation in our lives and in the world around us. This is also the element of wholeness about which we seem to know the least—but it is perhaps the most important piece to becoming the whole people we are made to be.

LIVE BY THE SPIRIT

We are Spirit-beings, made in God's image. We live by and for God. We don't deify things in this world like animists or pantheists. We don't live by our beauty, brains or bucks. Nor by our positions, possessions or by people we know. And not by animalistic urges or by mental philosophies or religions. God is Spirit, and when it comes down to the simple truth, we must worship him as such. He is the invisible force that leads us closer and closer to wholeness in this lifetime, and eventually, to perfect wholeness. This is the only way the Christian life gains momentum.

Christianity is not a natural religion that can be reduced to self-effort. When it comes to God, we can't give it the old college try; we can't be *The Little Engine That Could*. We don't believe we can ascend to heaven through our efforts of meditation, doing good or giving alms. Nor is our faith a mere mental effort assenting to what Jesus did historically. We don't believe people go to heaven because they have learned the magic prayer or decided to consider Jesus' claims as rational. Christianity is a relationship built on trust in Christ's forgiving and transforming love displayed at the cross and resurrection, and a life led by the Spirit of Wholly Jesus.

In Galatians 5:16, Paul urges his readers to live by this Spirit. The word is in the dative case, without a preposition, and could therefore be interpreted *in, with,* or *by the Spirit*. All three are possible.

To live in the Spirit emphasizes a location—a sphere. *Live in the realm or domain of the Spirit.* This is akin to Jesus' command to *abide in Him*. Living *by* the Spirit accents the means by which we live. It is through dependency on his strength and guidance that we live. *With* the Spirit emphasizes relationship. We are to walk in step with the Spirit. Paul actually states this in Galatians 5:25, when he says we are walking and living in his presence.

All three prepositions reveal the depth of what it means to be Spirit-people, living with, in and by the Spirit of God. We are pneumatic beings; without the Spirit we are broken and ineffective. A quick glance at the New Testament reveals the truth of this statement.

In Romans 8:9, Paul reminds us that we are controlled, not by our sinful nature, but by the Spirit. Not only do we live by the Spirit, but it is also by the Spirit that we put to death the misdeeds of the body (Romans 8:13). We now live under the influence of the Spirit (Ephesians 5:18). We pray and even love in the Spirit (Colossians 1:8). The Apostle Peter writes that the Spirit has given us everything we need to live the new, transformed life (2 Peter 1:3). For the believer, the Spirit is an empowering, life-giving, transforming person in whom we now live.

The history of humankind has been the history of power adaptation. Ancient man went from dragging stones over rolling logs to using carts on wheels drawn by horse and ox. Modern man has advanced from hydro-power and wind-power to solar-power and nuclear-power. Early on, humans realized that we, by ourselves, did not have the pxhysical power to do what we could imagine. In the same way, the transformed life described in Scripture and imagined in our minds is too great for our human effort. It is beyond self-help. We need an outside wind blowing through us to get us to our destination.

We can imagine transformed human beings looking like God in character. We can imagine bodies, marriages and families restored in love. We can imagine justice, the elimination of poverty and a world so transformed that the governments are submitted to the kingdom of God. But it is beyond our power to sustain this. We must rely on the power of the Wholly Spirit.

Yet, our reliance is not passive. Our will engages the Spirit's guidance and we must then follow. The command to live by the Spirit is not given to God to do for us. But it is given to us, that we might grab the hand of the Spirit and keep in step with him. Our "Yes, Lord" to the Spirit's leadership engages the power that spoke the world into being. Our "yes" expresses our dependency as well as our position of reflection, and it acknowledges that we are not the source of wholeness.

When we live by the Spirit we operate under a new default. The old default of our human system is sin and in that state we fulfill the desires of the sinful nature. But Wholly Jesus offers us a new default as we walk by his Spirit. As we do, the new default overrides the old and we bear the fruit of the Spirit instead of the fruit of the flesh.

LIVING IN THE PAINTING

For the most part, we objectify life. We stand on the outside looking in. Even worse, sometimes we deify objects in our lives, obsessing over them as if these things were gods. Wholly Jesus offers to bring about a transformation whereby each aspect of our lives is lived out, not merely observed. We don't cease to be human—we don't become enlightened humans or super humans—we become fully human.

Many times when I paddle out for an afternoon surf session, I experience what this means. In the early evening summer hours, it feels like time stands still. The water is warm, the setting sun is bright, and the August south-swells are crystal clear with bright orange garibaldi fish swimming below.

Then as the sun rests beyond the horizon, the sky bursts with color. The oranges and purples are reflected in the water where I am floating. It is then that I realize once more that I am in a painting. I am not standing on the cliff looking at the sunset and corduroy swells in the water below. I am in the painting, the colors encompass me, and in this painting is how I want to live.

THE WHOLLY FRUIT OF THE SPIRIT

There are several places in scripture where the Apostle Paul depicts the character of the transformed life. Perhaps most familiar are the nine characteristics used to describe this new life, called the fruit of the Spirit. These qualities are certainly not exhaustive, but they give us a taste of what the character of an image bearer is meant to be.

There are nine fruits Paul mentions. The first three describe our intrapersonal experience as we live in the Spirit. The next six describe our interpersonal approach to others. But all nine are there for others to pick and enjoy. Fruit is never simply for the plant to enjoy but for the passersby to pick, taste and enjoy. Fruit is also how the plant spreads its seeds (John 17).

The first three are *love, joy and peace*. Love is the premier fruit. God is love. We love because he first loved us. This love is both vertical toward God and horizontal toward others.

Love. The word is the familiar Greek word, *agape*. Although this term has been oversimplified, it is safe to say that the New Testament writers increasingly used this term to refer to divine love: God's love for us and the love we have for others. It is a love that is not grounded in the value of the object but in the nature of the subject—God, himself.

It is into this love that Wholly Jesus invites his followers to enter. It is the love of the father toward the prodigal son, the loving forgiveness of Jesus to the woman caught in adultery, the loving touch of Jesus toward the man with leprosy, and the loving tears of Jesus at Lazarus' tomb before he raised him from the dead. Living in the Wholly Spirit and bearing this love for others is certainly living inside the painting of life—the fruit is more vibrant and delicious than any other. It is this extraordinary taste of God's love that draws us, and others, nearer to him. It is a transforming fruit.

Joy. Joy is the next fruit Paul uses to describe our character. God is not only love, but he is also the happiest of all beings. Many can't imagine Jesus with a smile because the movies we see generally depict a grave face. But joy is a hallmark of God.

Paul, in fact, spent an entire letter on the subject of joy. Although he himself was writing from prison, he invites the Philippians to join him in the joy-filled life. It is a place where our trust in God's love overcomes the roller-coaster, ups and downs of life. It is a spiritual place of confidence that allows us to place checkmate on life. Whether circumstances serve up leaders who operate from good motives or bad (Philippians 1:15-18), in wealth or poverty (Philippians 4:12) or life or death (Philippians 1:18-21), we can bear the fruit of joy because our life is found in the risen Jesus. Paul did not live "under" the circumstances, but in the Wholly Spirit of Jesus.

Peace. Peace in the Western world is thought of primarily as tranquility or the cessation of war. The parent with three busy, laughing, screaming, running children wants some peace at the end of the day. The protesters of war want peace. But the peace Paul is describing is beyond these limitations. The word in Hebrew is *shalom* which is close to the word *wholeness, integration* or *well-being*. Today, people in the streets of Jerusalem still greet one another with, "How is your peace?" It holds much the same meaning as asking someone, "Are you well?"

Wholly Jesus is the Prince of Peace. Jesus said, "Peace I leave with you; my peace I give you. I do not give to you as the world gives"

(John 14:27). His bigger-than-this-world peace is a fruit we bear as we are transformed into his image. From this fruit are sown seeds of peace outwardly, through us.

***

The next three fruits are *patience, kindness, and goodness.* These are largely outward graces that the believer extends toward others. Perhaps we might say these fruits are primarily for others to taste and enjoy.

Patience. Patience is the fruit we extend toward those who aggravate or irritate us, or what we exhibit toward situations that frustrate us. The fruit of patience creates a buffer zone in our lives, where there is a sizable cushion between the failed plays of life and our reactions. We often think of ourselves as very patient people and we only lose our patience around very obnoxious and irritating people. But while we are waiting for the rest of the population to become more pleasant, we are the ones who need to grow in patience.

The old English word for "patience" is *longsuffering* (*macrothumia*). Most understand the meaning of *macro* to be *large or wide,* and *thumia* to mean *suffering.* So macrothumia means *large suffering* or to *suffer long.* It is in times when someone is irritating us or circumstances are causing us to suffer that the person in sync with the Wholly Spirit bears the fruit of patience. In contrast, a *microthumia* person is short-fused and explodes easily. It's tough to be around these kinds of people. We walk on eggshells. We wonder when they are going to explode again. Fortunately, as we walk in the Spirit, he changes our microthumia to macrothumia. And we need this to happen—I'll be the first to admit it.

My wife and I recently visited Disneyland and I had a bad case of microthumia. It peaked on the "Indiana Jones" ride. We had the "blessing" of two hysterical teenage girls sitting behind us who wanted to make the ride a screaming, obnoxious adventure for everyone. They had obviously ridden on the ride many times, so they began screaming before the ride even started. I'm talking blood-curdling screaming. They were only 24 inches behind my ears.

All throughout the ride they were screaming, "Oh my gosh, it's dark. Oh my gosh, we're turning left. Oh my gosh, the rock is falling on us..." They persisted with their "Oh my goshes," which were only interspersed with blood-curdling screams. The entire ride I was talking to myself, saying, "This is not going to get to me. I am enjoying the ride. They are not bothering me. I'm so chilled. I am having so much fun."

Finally, when my microthumia was spent, I went from thinking, "This does not effect me" to "How can I get back at them without being arrested at the end of the ride?" I decided to enter into their fun and scream my brains out, too. At the perfect moment while we banked a turn, I whipped around to face the girls and let out a blood curdling scream, interspersed with, "Oh my gosh, it's DARK! Oh my gosh, we're turning LEFT. Oh my GOSH!" These poor gals were suddenly terrified and became quiet throughout the rest of the ride.

As we hopped off the ride, I said to them, "Hey, that was a lot of fun, wasn't it?" They said, "Yeah, but we didn't know if you were angry or just having fun?" I said, "Oh, I was just entering into the game." But as I walked away I thought, "No, I wasn't. I was getting them back. I was thoroughly impatient." Clearly, I need to grow in patience.

Kindness. Kindness is related to patience. My act at Disneyland was neither kind nor patient. The two are twins. If a person isn't kind, they are usually harsh or judgmental. Sadly, there is a strong correlation between religious commitment and being judgmental. A recent Barna Group survey found that a vast majority of the mainstream population thinks of Christians as being judgmental.[1] The church definitely has an image problem.

Goodness. Goodness is a straightforward concept. It tastes just as you think it should. It's a word or a deed that's good toward somebody else. We all know the meaning of good weather, good food and good vacations. We all like good things but what this needy world desperately needs is good people.

The remaining fruits are *faithfulness, gentleness,* and *self-control.*

Faithfulness. Faithfulness is probably understood best by two contemporary terms: reliability and integrity. It means what we say and what we do are the same thing. We're not perfect but increasingly reliable. It's what a boss or manager is always looking for in an employee. It's what makes marriages, friendships and partnerships work. Though our righteousness is built on Jesus' faithfulness, it is his desire to now cultivate faithfulness in us. It is a fruit that tastes sweet to a world full of hidden agendas.

Gentleness. In this world, we have misunderstood gentleness to mean someone who is slump-shouldered, doesn't have an opinion and is mousy—in other words, a pushover. Gentleness is better translated as humility: knowing you could be the first one to speak or the first in line, but you decide against it because you would rather honor others. Instead of being a "Here I am" kind of person, you are a "There you are" kind of person. Gentleness is strength under control.

Self-control. A better way to describe this final fruit is self-mastery. I'm told the word *control* doesn't ever appear in scripture without the word *self.* It teaches us an important lesson. Here's the problem: if a conference for believers was offered on the subject of "Self-Control", very few people would come. Why? Because we are not that excited about controlling ourselves.

This is at the core of the matter. The final fruit brings us full circle to the core of advancing the kingdom of God. If I bear the fruit of self-control, it is because I am yielded to the king of the kingdom. If I don't, it is doubtful how surrendered I am. The same is true of each fruit. They are not gathered as separate crops but harvested in clusters. To bear them in greater supply is to become more whole. The fruits of the Wholly Spirit are the Heavenly Gardener's offer to a broken and hungry world. "Taste and see," he says, "that I am good" (Psalm 34:8). The only way one tastes this fruit is as it blooms in us.

BE FILLED WITH THE WHOLLY SPIRIT

The pragmatist must ask, "How does this happen? How do we continue to be filled with the Spirit?" For certain, Christianity is not magic. While we cannot separately measure the efficacy of each spiritual discipline such as prayer, Scripture reading and solitude, each discipline, when used in faith, places us in a posture of dependency on the Spirit whereby we might continue to transform and bear fruit. Others writers have exhaustively mined this subject, but I offer several that seem to be most effective in my life.

I have discovered that *giving thanks* renews my mind and fills me with dependency on God's Spirit. When I awake overwhelmed with stress, I won't allow myself to think or intercede until I have first thanked God for a minimum of ten minutes. I thank him for everything, from flowers to people, from blessings to unresolved issues. Often miracles take place in those short ten minutes when I experience a sense of God's immediate presence.

My thinking is transformed as I begin to see what is right rather than what is wrong with the world. I agree in my spirit that God is sovereign and is already working in this world. I move from fretting and demanding to depending and resting on him. I return to joining the beautiful lilies of the field of which Jesus spoke. Ultimately, I become a child dependent upon a Father.

To convince yourself of the importance of thanksgiving, do a concordance study on the word. You will be overwhelmed with the amount of thanks that Paul alone offers to God; it was a way of life for him. Prayer is often mixed with thanks (Ephesians 1:16; Colossians 1:3; 4:2; 1 Thessalonians 1:2; 2 Timothy 1:3; Philemon 4) and thanks is commanded of us (Colossians 3:17; 1 Thessalonians 5:18). It's a way of living in the painting of God's reality and it clearly helps us see the fingerprints of Wholly Jesus in one's life.

Praise and singing to God is another discipline that needs to be reignited in the church community. Most expositors interpret Ephesians 5:19 as the expressive result of being filled, but it is also the precursor to becoming filled. When we speak and sing the truths of God privately or publicly, the Spirit is released more fully in our lives.

Unfortunately, the day of mass produced worship has created an increasingly passive audience that only listens to others singing. We drive along or sit in church listening to the singing of others. While these are uplifting exercises, there is need for our will to be engaged. We, not the digital singer, must declare God's worth. Whether it is audible or not, we must agree with what is being sung. This makes it a potentially transformational moment. Matt Redman expresses this well in his song, *Heart of Worship.*[2]

I enjoy being with my friends from Nepal who sing constantly to themselves throughout the day. It seems they are always overflowing with the Spirit. It is this dependency that has carried them through threats from radical Hindus, Maoists and government soldiers. It is the Spirit that allows them to plant churches in such rugged terrain and under such adverse circumstances.

Although, Prem Predham is now with the Lord, he experienced prison situations similar to that of the Apostle Paul. Just as Paul and Silas sang in prison in Philippi, Prem, too, worshiped many times behind his prison walls. The presence of Wholly Jesus would be with him in prison. Many guards became believers. He was transferred twelve times throughout the country to various prisons because the guards were converted and became his brothers. Little did the government realize they were seeding the entire country with the Gospel.

In the final analysis, praise is simply recognizing what is of ultimate value. It is our honest response to a good, faithful, loving maker and savior. To do anything else is dishonest. Praise is truth. It is a true reflection of the Wholly image in which we are made.

When I *study God's Word* I am encouraged, reminded and corrected by truth. Though I can feel lost in this hectic life, in the Word I rediscover true north on the compass. My mind is renewed and I see things once again from God's perspective. Though the early church believers did not have their own personal Bibles, it is clear that the songs being sung to each other described in Ephesians 5:19 are the words of truth. David, the psalter, often focused on the value of God's Word (Psalm 119). As I respond in faith and love to his truth, I am filled with his Spirit.

As I am in *fellowship,* I am encouraged and filled with his spirit. A water drop alone is at risk of being evaporated, but amidst other water drops, it has the potential of becoming a river. We need each other and it is in the gathering that we are refueled. Christianity was never intended to be an individualistic expedition. In America we attempt to live individualistic, autonomous lives and our faith does not work well in such an environment because self-reliance is not truth.

When I *resist temptation* or experience God's forgiveness, a fresh filling occurs and I am refueled in the Spirit. In these moments there is an empowerment and a sense of victory. Territory that was once held by the devil is relinquished to the kingdom of God. In *Pilgrim's Progress*, Christian said to Apollyon, "Beware of what you do; for I am in the King's highway, the way of holiness; therefore take heed to yourself."[3] It was with the Word of God that the enemy was defeated. After Jesus overcame the devil with the Word of God, he returned in the power of the Spirit (Luke 4:14). Though we pray to not experience temptation, when we do and overcome it, we are empowered.

There is a place for laying hands on each other to be filled with the Spirit—as long as it engages the person's will. It is not magic. Certainly the laying on of hands was part of the initiation described in the book of Acts. A believer repented, was baptized in water and often had someone who "laid hands" on the initiate, asking God to fill them with the Spirit. Those vessels were filled with the Spirit and then prayed for those who were empty. James Dunn, in his seminal work, *The Baptism of the Holy Spirit*, rightly calls the laying on of hands for the Spirit part of the initiation experience.[4] But what does one do who has never heard of being filled with the Spirit or has been distant from God for sometime and returns to God? It would seem appropriate for the church in these instances as well to lay hands on the person, asking Wholly Jesus to freshly fill them with his Spirit.

Through loving and giving ourselves away to others, we are refilled. As we respond in obedience to the Spirit, giving ourselves to others, we are refilled with the Spirit. Jesus made it clear that when we feed the poor and visit those in hospitals and prisons, we are actually feeding and visiting him; and will be rewarded as such. That is, Jesus is interconnected with us in such a way that what we do to others in his body, we do to him. Some of our most intimate, mystical, infilling experiences with the Spirit are not in the closet or in a church service but on the street, reaching out to others.

As we obey, we are filled with God's spirit. This looping effect has been discussed in the previous chapter. But it is in our "yes" to God's command (which is primarily to love others sacrificially) that we are refilled with his spirit. The connection between the command to be filled in Ephesians 5:18 and how we are to live toward others in love is clear: we open the valve of the Spirit in our lives when we obediently love others.

It is a remarkable thing to realize we have God, by his Spirit, living inside of us. Jesus says this is the ultimate gift (Luke 11:11-13). As a good Father, God will not withhold this gift from us when we ask. And his desire is to have his Spirit overflowing in our lives like living water, refreshing our soul and the lives around us (John 7:37-38). Jesus said, *"If anyone is thirsty, let him come to me and drink. Whoever believes in me, as the Scripture has said, streams of living water will flow from within him."* It is wonderful to think that while we bear fruit ourselves, this living water can flow through us to water the seeds of God's image in others.

Ultimately, being filled with the Spirit is being near Jesus. It is me being his shadow, his image. It is his kingdom ruling in and through me. It is his wind in my sails, his breath on my face.

DON'T QUENCH OR GRIEVE THE SPIRIT

We have all heard the adjective "dead" used to describe a church. We have known believers who seemed to be alive in the Spirit then become lifeless. Each of us have known that sick feeling inside when we have done something to disappoint ourselves and God. The Apostle Paul uses two words that may best describe the diminished presence of the Spirit: *grieving and quenching*.

I don't know if there was much difference between quenching and grieving the Spirit in the mind of the Apostle Paul. One could argue that *to quench* means *to put a fire out* or *to turn off a hose*. It is to stop something that is already happening or say "no" to an ongoing request of the Spirit. *To grieve* changes the metaphor: the picture now is a person who is hurt or disappointed.

The Spirit is a person who is affected by what we do. As extraordinary as that seems, God is a person who feels what we do. It is his choice to have that type of relationship with us. Human descriptions of God are not for the purpose of dismissing God's reactions to us, but just the opposite: they help us understand him. Our behavior, though known by God's foreknowledge, still pleases or grieves him.

The believer understands that he or she must remain filled with the Spirit to make this Christian life work—that means not deflating ourselves by grieving or quenching the Spirit. We must live in a dependent relationship with the Spirit.

Sometimes I wonder if the sticky, shameful feeling we get when we sin isn't just our conscience, but actually the Spirit grieving inside of us. I wonder if we actually feel something of what he feels. It is that inner tension and uneasiness that helps to keep us on the straight and narrow. While I don't fully understand the dynamics as it relates to the Spirit inside us, I know I don't like the feeling of sin.

We don't fully understand what happens in the Spiritual realm when we sin and grieve the Spirit, but it would also seem that unresolved sin gives the devil a inroad into our lives (Ephesians 4:26-27). And answers to our prayers may actually be hindered in this rebellious state (1 Peter 3:7). There is no telling the great damage we do to ourselves and others when we grieve and quench the Spirit. It may be that we actually harm or shrink our souls in that we aren't able to long for and enjoy God's presence as we might have otherwise. It is through confession that we are forgiven and then refilled with the Spirit.

THE IMAGE

How much of this transformation can we taste in this life? We've spoken of the already-but-not-yet tension we experience, but how does that relate to our becoming whole? How much of God's face can be ours in this life? How much of the Wholly Spirit can fill us? How much can God use us in this life to touch others with his nature? Such questions are like asking an Indy car driver, "How fast can this baby go?" The right answer would be, "Hop in and let's see."

Philosophers, theologians, dictators, behavioral scientists, poets and pop singers have speculated as to the nature of the perfect person. What does he or she look like? What characteristics make this person complete? Nietzsche had his "Overman" or Superman who he envisioned would overcome the power of the soul, the power of pity and the belief in the afterlife. Pop culture has its Jolie-Pitts who exhibit in some way ideal people. But everyone falls short in some way.

I've found that even Christians are confused about what the fully transformed, wholly human looks like in this life. The Biblical definition pivots on the *Imago Dei*. But what does that look like? As a person approaches Jesus' image, what qualities can we expect to possess and how is this transformation achieved and maintained?

It is the character of Jesus we want to reflect, and one of the purest, most encompassing statements about Jesus' nature:

> The Word became flesh and made his dwelling among us. We have seen his glory, the glory of the One and Only, who came from the Father, full of grace and truth. (John 1:14)

Here we see a whole person, God in the flesh, showing us the pure face of the Father. In Jesus, the earthly savior, we witnessed the glory of God. He lived and "pitched his tent" among us. And the two ingredients we saw most were *grace* and *truth*.

BECOMING A KING

Someone has said, "It's one thing to be called a king, it's quite another to become the king you've been called to be." The same could be said of us as humans: "It's one thing to be called a human. It's quite another to become the human being you've been called to be"—to become the image of God.

David, the shepherd boy, was anointed by Samuel to be king. He had been tested by the bear, by the lion and by the monster Goliath, but was about to be tested like never before. Ultimately, it is in the testing that we are transformed. It is in the becoming that we are transformed toward wholeness. In these situations, two things either rise to the surface or fall short: *grace* and *truth*.

There was a short time in David's life when everything was coming up roses. He was the court minstrel for King Saul, best friend to Prince Jonathan, and a military commander with tremendous success. He was a rock star who had shot up the charts.

It's one thing to be a godly person when you're getting everything you want. But what do we do when we think we know the will of God and it isn't happening? David knew he was ultimately to be the king, yet once Saul became jealous of him and attempted to kill him, David made like a jackal and went into hiding. It was during these 13 years that he became the king he had been called to be.

David's story in the desert is the nightmare that many have lived. Like Theresa of Avila once said to God, "If this is how you treat your friends, no wonder you don't have many." It is in the fire that the dross is burned away and we become refined, pure gold.

After a dozen difficult years of testing, it is in the village of Ziglag that we see David emerge with God-like character beyond that of a good leader. The situation at Ziglag was bleak. David and his fighting men had returned from being rejected by the Philistine army, only to find their village burned and the women and children kidnapped. Discouraged and bitter, these normally loyal men turned on David and began to plot his death. David, in this broken trough, had lost his family, the palace comfort, the friendship of Jonathan, the prestige as commander, the future kingship, his family and now possibly his life. It was at this all-time low that David's refining was most intense.

David is not alone in this fire of proven character. The testing is the temptation to believe the same devil that was in the garden, to believe that God is holding out on us and that he is not faithful and loving. Those who believe in God's goodness during this dark night emerge on the other side with God's character.

No one is perfect this side of heaven, but brokenness is somehow key to transformation. I often ask a person who is being interviewed for a pastoral position to tell me their story of brokenness. If they don't have a David-story in a small way, I fear that their theology is not connected to life.

It seems odd to say, but in God's economy our brokenness refines us. Our disabilities enable us in a powerful way. It seems that in this broken world, grace is often more evident on the heels of disgrace, and truth is often more evident on the heels of falsehood. Perhaps we might say that in this way the kingdom of God breaks through on both sides of human existence. It is the light in the darkest hour and brighter than the light of day. A city on a hill cannot be hidden, no matter the hour.

chapter eleven

Risk, Sacrifice and Wholly Transformation

While women weep, as they do now, I'll Fight; while little children go hungry, as they do now, I'll Fight; while men go to prison, in and out, in and out, as they do now, I'll Fight; while there is a poor lost girl upon the streets, while there remains one dark soul without the light of God, I'll Fight, I'll fight to the very end!

— William Booth

A s a young convert, I didn't know how to integrate my new found faith with my day-to-day life. I was in a cover band and we played every weekend. My new Christian friends from church said I needed to quit the band and stop playing "secular" music. I had never heard the term before. They quoted some verse from the Bible, "Come out from among them and be ye separate." Not knowing any Scripture yet, it sounded pretty impressive and at the same time confusing. "Come out of Babylon," they said, "don't be unequally yoked." It all sounded so heavy. Cautiously, I determined to do nothing until my new teacher, Wholly Jesus, told me what to do.

I organized a band meeting the next week to tell them I had become a Christian. I wanted to be up front and thought that's what a Christian was supposed to do. It was a dark day as we sat around someone's parent's living room. The band members were somber, worried and shocked with the news, as if I had just told them I had cancer. There was no "congratulations". Not even a "Cool, man."

They were processing it all: Mark Foreman ... a Christian—two concepts that previously didn't go together. How were these two ideas going to integrate in real life?

Instantly, everyone wanted to know if it meant I was quitting the band. I told them I had no plans to do so, but I said, "I would not leave my Lord off the stage. He goes with me everywhere." "Fair enough," they said. We had four months of gigs scheduled and I knew I was good for those. But I was not prepared for the unexpected source of harassment, and it wasn't from my band mates.

Musicians and others in the church continually hassled me about the band. I should quit right away, they said, and become a part of one of the bands forming in the church. Again, like a broken record, they told me to "come out of the world and don't be unequally yoked."

It didn't make any sense. Why play in a band that evangelizes about Jesus inside a church? My band was already well connected in the local music scene among people who needed to hear about God's love. I said to them, "It is the outside community that needs Jesus. Why evangelize the choir?" I told them I was in a position to be a light by playing the mainstream gigs. Still, they insisted I was compromising myself by playing secular music in secular venues.

Soon the guitar player and singer, Dave, became a believer. It was dramatic. He quit all his drugs and began attending church with me. We began to write songs about the Lord and share those songs with the band. We even sang our songs at clubs and school dances on our breaks below the stage, unplugged for anyone who wanted to listen. The ensuing discussions with people at the gigs were amazing. But the tension was building.

I think it was the Doobie Brothers' *Jesus Is Just Alright* that pushed matters over the edge. Dave and I taught the song to the band and we began covering it in three-part harmony at every gig. But the other band members finally expressed that they were uncomfortable singing about Jesus. They admitted that they would prefer that we return to a psychedelic repertoire about love, sex and drugs, and leave out the Jesus stuff. They even quoted Scripture, "For everything there is a season."

I was prepared for this and I calmly reminded them that Jesus goes with me everywhere. If he couldn't come to the gigs then I would not be coming. We finished up the remaining gigs and buried the band. That summer Dave and I hitchhiked up the coast to Oregon, singing in coffee houses, staying in halfway houses and sleeping under bridges. Little did we know at the time that this music issue was bumping up against a deep nerve in the church and how it related to culture.

BELIEVERS AT RISK

Believers are in a difficult situation. On the one hand, we are to follow Jesus down the path of internal transformation, becoming new people. On the other hand, we are to follow him down the path of outward transformation, bringing the message and the life of the kingdom into the world. But because this world is broken, following him into the world may put us at risk. We may be misunderstood, persecuted or exposed to temptations. This then places the internal work at risk. There is the real possibility of being tempted to return to the godless life that we left while attempting to help others. While we are behind enemy lines, believers are always at risk.

Certainly recovering addicts need to stay away from the places of temptation until they can become strong in their new life. Alcoholics should stay away from liquor stores, bank robbers from banks, pot heads from their old friends and perhaps habitual liars from talking at all. But is it possible to escape the risk of being corrupted by the world while following Jesus "into all the world?"

Believers are not alone in their risk. Doctors and nurses risk catching the patient's disease. Narcotic officers are tempted to participate in the very trafficking they are trying to stop. Government officials are tempted to sellout their integrity for bribes while serving their country to legislate justice. All are susceptible to the very thing they want to transform. But luckily for us, a divine leader has gone before us.

This was the very risk the Son of God took when he came to this earth. By becoming one of us, he risked catching our contagious sinful behavior: "He was tempted at all points just as we are" (Hebrews

4:15). He not only died for our sin, he was also at risk to actually sin himself. Temptation is not temptation unless there is the real possibility of actually yielding to it. We sometimes like to think of Jesus as one who was impervious to actually sinning. This is not true. He was just as we are, just as susceptible, just as vulnerable, but without sin. From the manger to the cross, heaven's Prince was at risk.

The risk is real. But we can't retreat. Retreating would be to withdraw from the very world God loves. Besides, the idea of withdrawing from society is a temptation itself. This is an ironic temptation. In the name of being righteous, some stop following Jesus into society. And the more we have to risk, the stronger this temptation becomes.

Put simply, it's the temptation to play it safe, to not risk it all by continuing to follow Jesus into untransformed places. The temptation is to protect my time, reputation, spouse, children, career, income and retirement for the "sake of the Gospel." Further, we can actually use God and the concept of righteousness as an excuse to not radically follow Christ into the dark corners of life. We back off from the world while quoting Scripture about purity and safety to support our lack of involvement.

The Pharisees had their excuses. Jesus' cavalier behavior with tax collectors, prostitutes and sinners threatened them. They had too much to lose to follow Jesus to Golgotha. They must have internally asked, "What would my friends in the Sanhedrin say? People might misunderstand." So leaders like Nicodemus met with Jesus secretly at night to avoid the gossip and ridicule.

It's easy for the protection of what is ours to become one of our highest values of life and to build scriptures around our protectionism and separatism. There is always a verse out of context to support anyone's thinking. Meanwhile, Wholly Jesus unswervingly moves forward, getting his hands dirty and asking us to do the same.

The history of cultural fundamentalism is wonderful and difficult all at once. I say "cultural" because there is a distinction between the fundamentals of the faith found in Scripture and the culture that emerged in the 20th century around fundamentalism. I believe in the fundamentals, but I don't believe in its culture anymore.

Fundamentalism was birthed as a reaction to liberalism. Liberal scholars at the close of the 19th century stopped believing in Jesus. Modernity (rationalism and empiricism) had become fully ripe. Hence, the virgin birth, Jesus' healings and miracles, his sacrifice for our sins and his physical resurrection wasn't rational. As they whittled away the fundamentals of the faith, there was not much left on the stick of faith to distinguish their brand of Christianity from any other natural religion. But to their credit, liberals continued in the trans-forming-culture-path of the evangelicals of the 19th century: caring for the poor, the sick, the abused and the planet. Some, as missionar-ies, even risked their lives for social reform. Fundamentalists reacted to the liberal's agenda and derogatorily called it the "social gospel."

In turn, the fundamentalists turned their back on their evangeli-cal-social-reform roots and went solo, preaching and teaching only the words of the Gospel. Not wanting to be viewed as a liberal, they ceased to transform hospitals and prisons, and to feed and defend the poor. They withdrew from society, only studying, teaching and defending the Bible.

The church became a safe castle with ever thickening walls to pro-tect itself from the sin of society. "Come out and be ye separate" was its cry. To be fair, every now and then the castle drawbridge would drop and the knights would ride out once again for revival and cru-sades. These usually lasted a week in a sawdust-floor tent or public arena. Wonderfully, people were saved and healed. But once the week was over, the church expected sinners to come back into the castle with them and be "separate" once again.

At that time, certain parts of culture were considered more defil-ing than others. Hollywood with its music and movies, Washington with its shady politics, New York with its greed for power and money, and Paris with its shocking fashion were all anathema. It was from these parts of culture that the church withdrew. But it also withdrew from the needy sectors of society because that had the appearance of the social gospel. The church justified this with apocalyptic language like, "It's all going to burn. If the building is burning down, you try to save the people in the building, not the building." The heroes of the church did not study and prepare to enter any of these dens of wickedness, but instead became preachers outside the dens. There was good news for the soul but not always for society.

Fundamentalist culture was a separatist culture misguided in its pursuit of wholeness. It did not know how to "love not the world," and at the same time follow a God who "so loved the world." Although the church "loved the world" weekly by giving an altar call within the church walls, it mistakenly thought that it was right to keep the world outside. It was not astute enough to realize that the world (*cosmos*), as the apostle John meant it, was also inside the church; that "the lust of the flesh, the lust of the eyes and pride" were in the church as well as in mainstream culture.

I was raised on the social gospel. I was taught to be a good Samaritan in every aspect of life. When friends of mine and I came to faith in Jesus, I thought we were the ones, the Jesus Movement, destined to change the world.

Before becoming a believer, I had worn a black armband protesting the Vietnam War, I ate fresh ground wheat and other health foods, I cared about the planet, I fed the poor and believed in civil rights. Mine was the generation that distrusted the establishment of power and we were destined in our idealism to change the world. Now with Jesus at my side, there was no telling what might happen.

Unfortunately, little happened socially. Just as the hippies became yuppies, I became a modern day separatist. Although I kept my rock-n-roll for Jesus and wore my hair long, I followed the previous generation, retreating into the safe castle of the church.

I didn't worry too much about war; after all, there "would be wars and rumors of wars." I didn't fret too much about the poor; after all, "the poor you have with you always." And I didn't care about justice issues; after all, there were injustices and slavery in the 1st century as well, and the early believers lived through them. Besides, Jesus would put it right at the second coming, not now. I didn't care about culture in general. I ignored the arts, unless it was making mugs with IXTHUS's on them. I ignored music unless it contained lyrics that were preachy or worshipful. I ignored politics, until abortion became an issue. Then I started voting and the Moral Majority guided me. The only issues that were moral were abortion and sexual preference. Somehow other issues such as justice, civil rights, poverty, the health of our planet and war were neither moral nor important.

How did I and an entire generation who believed in saving the planet, defending civil rights, helping the poor and stopping war, unplug and give society away to others who had a different moral compass? It was a combination of the hippie "drop out" mentality and separatist religion. My generation was primarily concerned with saving souls, protecting our children from the world and leaving the society to fend for itself. I was not responsible for the world. In the name of "not loving the world," I and my generation gave the world away. I studied my Bible, taught my children and waited for the rapture. Whatever concern I previously had for this world was lost into cultural fundamentalism.

J. E. Orr, the famous historian on revival, challenged a few of us in a small meeting in Forest Home near the end of the 1970's, telling us that the Jesus Movement wasn't a revival because there had been no significant change in society. He rattled off statistics and antidotes from the First and Second Great Awakening to show us the difference. From those revivals cultural institutions were drastically transformed. But with the Jesus Movement, while we had effectively evangelized, we had only accomplished the opposite, withdrawing from all cultural institutions and leaving no mark on the outside world.

My understanding of the integration of Scripture and culture was underdeveloped, but I meant well. And though we may not have been a revival according to J. E. Orr, many lives were transformed. Souls were saved, many were delivered from drugs, marriages were restored, and morals were shaped. My life and my family were changed. There were many standout exceptions to our separatism such as the Salvation Army whose approach to a person's salvation was holistic. And brave men such as Chuck Smith reached out to the hippies, while the rest of the church was unwilling to touch them. Franklin Graham's Samaritan's Purse and other Christian NGO's began holistically serving the poor around the world. But in our daily lives, we just didn't know how to exist in this world. To our credit, many souls were saved and promised heaven, but to our shame, we restricted our role as salt and light to the world. We were products of our time.

Mistakenly, we were modern day Amish. Although we thought

we were relevant with our long hair and music, still we withdrew from the world just like the Amish. Although there were exceptions, for the most part we solely focused on saving souls. To our credit, many souls were saved and promised heaven, but to our shame, we restricted our role as salt and light.

When I began to wake up, two entire decades had past. Like Rip Van Winkle opening his eyes, I soon realized society had moved on. I didn't know any of the hit songs, any name or issue in Washington, any sports figures, any trends in business, the arts, philosophy or literature. I was a modern day caveman.

CHRIST AND CULTURE

Thankfully I remembered a book from seminary by Richard Niebuhr entitled *Christ and Culture*. Without embracing Niebuhr's theology in total, I found what I had been looking for. Two of his five positions toward culture reflected our present tension: *Christ against culture* and *Christ transforming culture*.[1]

I realized I had been the Christ-against-culture person. I had been in a culture war. I was against Washington, New York and Hollywood … against society itself. I was too naive not to realize that church has a culture, too, and that God will judge all culture. A wise missionary to the Navajo people once cautioned me that all culture is under the judgment of God, including church culture—be it liberal, evangelical or fundamentalist.

Niebuhr was clear to point out that there is no perfect interface with culture. The church has varied in her approach over the centuries. But *Christ transforming culture* seemed to be the antidote to our separatism. But how would we even begin to tackle such an assignment? How does the church transform culture with the salt and light of Christ?

The *Christ against culture* is a negative, suspicious, closed, protectionist, defensive culture. It is not a safe place for someone with a lot of questions. The separatist church tends to circle the wagons and shoot at anything that is perceived a threat. The separatist culture does two things that are harmful:

1. It disengages the church from society, muting its affect as salt and light. God's plan for us to reflect his image to a broken society is dulled at best, and lost at worst. All aspects of culture and society desperately need to taste the fruit of the Wholly Spirit and see the face of their Creator. Someone will always impact culture but sadly, if the church exists in a separatist culture, the influence won't come from a believer. The church without its full mission is the first harm done, but the health of the church is also at risk when it turns inward.

2. The second harm is to the church itself. The church, like a team defending it's own goal, is forced to live on the defense, when it has little offense to penetrate the world. It develops a fearful, cautious, judgmental culture within its walls. Like a surrounded army, it shoots at anything that looks suspicious, judging, gossiping, even slandering those it thinks may be a threat to its "godly" castle.

These environments can be quite damaging emotionally to those wanting to discover the wholeness Jesus brings. On the surface, grace is taught, but underneath, the potential of rejection thrives with rigidity and judgment. Furthermore, it is all done with the utmost sincerity of following God. The church leaders have been deputized by Jesus to protect the church and the gospel, and they will move swiftly to reject anyone they perceive to be a threat. Cults are the extreme examples of this, but marginal sectarian/separatist churches often create a similar culture.

The irony is that this kind of hurtful church culture needs redemption and transformation just as much as the world. The kingdom values of Jesus need to enter the church. I have counseled many believers wounded from such emotional abuse. The church walls seem to gradually grow thicker and thicker, disallowing people to easily come in and feel accepted, while also keeping members from easily going out into the community.

When countries have isolated themselves from the world, creating an us-against-them mentality, the citizens of that country have often suffered and paid dearly. The political leaders exert their energy spinning and managing the interpretation of information that goes in and out. Iran, North Korea and Venezuela are recent examples. In the same way, many have written about the emotional damage that has

happened within the extreme separatist churches that have rigidly
controlled their members in such "we/they" worlds.[2] Because of
unredeemed church culture, there are many who walk the streets as
victims of the church. Many want to say "yes" to Jesus but have
already said "no" to the church.

In contrast, *Christ transforming culture* creates a culture of
responsibility rather than escapism and protection. It is a team on the
offense. It understands its mission is not safety and protection, but
invasion and transformation. The risk that a believer might forget the
mission and get lost in culture is always there; but the risk is the same
in a separatist church culture. The critical difference is that the reward
of risk for the follower of Jesus in culture is transformation. The
reward for the follower safe in the church walls is merely more safety.

As opposed to the traditional "we/they" approach (*Christ
against culture*), *Christ transforming culture* takes a "we/we"
approach. Instead of simply standing against a sinful culture, the
church within culture learns to partner and work alongside the local
community bringing transformation in every way possible. This repo-
sitions the church from a black-and-white, apocalyptic worldview,
where the world is simply waiting to be judged and burned, to a
redeeming worldview, where the kingdom of heaven is restoring the
world through the people of the church. Once a we-we approach is
adopted, the church becomes the community's center for help, service, love and transformation, and the community becomes the
church's parish. But to accomplish this, the church must become wise
to the cultural pathways that have been given to us to travel on.

TRAVELING CULTURAL PATHWAYS

Our friends, Tom and Janet, took off for Peru in their mid-twen-
ties with their children. They moved into the jungles of the upper
Amazon, hoping to make contact with a hidden people group.
Disease, death, poverty, alligators, poisonous snakes, plants, insects
and hostile aboriginal people were all waiting for their arrival. My
friend Tom went risking his wife, his children and his own life. I ques-

tioned his actions. "God would never ask anyone to do that for him! Isn't safety the most important value? They must not be wise." Fifteen years later, I know what they lost and what they gained for Christ.

I have seen the personal film footage of the indigenous people making contact with Tom for the first time. It took years of patience and persistence. Tom and his Peruvian friends would leave gifts on the pathways that they found in the jungle. They moved into the jungle with their families to show the hidden people group that they meant no harm. They knew if only the men came into the jungle then the hidden people would interpret this as a sign of war. And if they carved their own jungle pathways, that too would be viewed as hostile. So they walked the existing pathways, leaving gifts, living with their families in huts, hoping and waiting for the day that eventually came.

This missionary posture of danger and traveling existing cultural pathways is accepted and praised by the separatist church when it comes to missionary work in other countries. But for some reason, a large portion of the church in America has taken an entirely different strategy at home. Unlike Paul who traveled the existing Roman roads, using the *lingua franca* of the day, capitalizing on his Roman citizenship, and arguing astutely on Mars Hill with the philosophers of Athens, this sort of church has separated, creating its own culture.

If we are going to not only win souls, but also holistically transform culture, we must be equally strategic. We must find the pathways that exist in our cultural jungles and not simply create our own "Christian" pathways. We must befriend the people of the land. We must spend an inordinate amount of time and energy on pre-evangelism, not simply evangelism. We must learn the language and the culture, and we must love the people. We must be prepared to help people medicinally, educationally, relationally, socially and commercially. We must become incarnate like Wholly Jesus. We must present the wholeness they crave in a way they understand.

RE-ENTERING CULTURE

Imagine that you are a 21st century missionary sailing up the coast of California for the first time. Like the 16th century explorer,

Juan Cabrillo, you are seeing the semi-desert golden coast of California for the first time. As you anticipate coming ashore, you look through your telescope at the fast-paced, un-aboriginal people racing on the Interstate 5 Freeway. How will you reach them? How will you bring transformation to them without changing the good and moral aspects of their culture? Will you build a hillside fort for protection from which you will drop strategic, artistically outdated flyers? Will you plant a church and gradually invite people to your services? Will you build a missionary compound? How will you do it?

If we were to adopt Tom and Janet's approach from the jungles of Peru, or the Apostle Paul's strategy, you would be looking for the pathways of these un-indigenous people. You could travel quicker and be more trusted if you knew these paths. To learn them, you must be with the people, asking them where they go, what they do, and on what cultural paths they travel. The astute cultural anthropologist would observe several paths that are common in the jungles of Western civilization. Upon these pathways, the people travel constantly; these pathways are the fabric of their civilization. It is on these pathways that the gifts of Wholly Jesus must be placed.

These pathways include government, education, technology, business, entertainment, the arts, sports, media and communication, religion, medicine/therapy and philanthropy. The jungle of Western civilization is thick and a missionary must learn these cultural ways in order to travel quickly and effectively. To meet and befriend the people, these pathways must become your pathways. To effect culture with the love and truth of Christ, these pathways must be yours— these pathways must be ours.

But this has not been the church's typical approach. Usually a church planter shows up in town and begins building a church. The planter allows the un-aboriginals to stay busy on their pathways while he or she is busy building the church. Like the Franciscans, the planter soon enlists the people to help him build his church. He ignores the existing cultural pathways because they are infected with the world and creates his own safe pathways of church sports, music, media and education. The result is that parallel worlds develop and never interfere with one another. Church is church. Culture is culture.

The people come out of culture to go to church. Often they don't see a Jesus who has much to do with culture because the planter ignored the pathways that existed. Church becomes a sacred space on the edge of society. The perception is that Wholly Jesus lives on the outskirts of "real life." To try to integrate church and culture at this point is difficult. It is hard to retrofit people's daily pathways with Jesus when it was not the church planter's original approach.

Traveling the existing cultural pathways must be part of the mission from the beginning. Each pathway must be both validated and boldly transformed. The kingdom of God is to enter all aspects of life and not merely exist on the edge of society. It is not an extracurricular activity practiced on weekends. It is at the heart of all we do.

Religion and philosophy has always been at the heart of culture, so for a church to be integrated with a culture is nothing new. Whether one looks to primitive or modern societies, animistic or atheistic, at the core of culture are one or more philosophies and religions. This is how civilizations are built. We must reclaim our rightful role as the hub of culture.

To effectively transform culture, a separatist approach will never work. The believers in that culture must become incarnate. They must travel in the veins of society, risking temptation and compromise, for the sake of loving the people with God's love. A game in sports cannot be won with a defense alone. The offense must move the ball forward.

In the end, in this way a culture is not only transformed by the salt and light of Wholly Jesus, but the church itself is stronger and healthier. It is the separatist church that ultimately becomes anemic.

WHOLLY EDUCATION

I am often asked to advise parents on how to raise their children, especially teenagers. One thing I always advise is for parents to take their youth on a stretching mission trip to some challenging part of the world. Take them to a township in South Africa, a Dhalit village in northern India, to a tsunami, tornado, flood or hurricane relief operation, to build a house in Tijuana, to work on a project alongside a poorer inner city church, or to a breadline in any downtown in America. Let them see *why* Jesus' truth is important. Take them to the edge of themselves, stretching their comfort zone, and it will suddenly click as to why Jesus came. If you raise your children to just be safe, they will become ineffective Christians. *Trying* to be good isn't good enough.

The cultured, stretched youth will understand why they need to study and pray, why they need fellowship, why they need to stay strong as believers—because their assignment in life is threatening and challenging. They will understand what it means to live in and, simultaneously, transform culture.

As parents and church leaders, we must ask ourselves, what is the goal of parenting and Christian education in general? If it is to raise children who are safe—heaven-bound, doctrine-knowing and never doing drugs, not having premarital sex or never smoking—then we should keep them outside society on a farm in Nebraska. But if the goal is to raise children who are salt and light—strong, legitimate threats to the kingdom of darkness—then we must use different tactics. Our training must include field trips where they see their parents and leaders doing the stuff Jesus did: feeding the poor, healing and visiting the sick in hospitals and nursing homes, working with prisoners, listening to discussions about Jesus with people who aren't like us in places that aren't comfortable.

Youth want to believe that Jesus is a radical who is out to transform this world. They intuitively know that there is something wrong with the tame Jesus of America's suburbs, the Jesus who is only interested in keeping us safe from the defilements of the world and getting souls too safely into heaven. The Jesus they read about in their Bibles is edgy, taking risks with God's love to the unlovely of society—that's the Jesus they want to follow. That's Wholly Jesus.

The modality of a church on the edge of society that is not involved in culture will not change society and runs the risk of irrelevancy. A friend, traveling the entertainment pathway, once called me from a studio in Hollywood and said, "They're not against Christians like I thought. It's worse. We're irrelevant." But that is because we have made ourselves irrelevant by not loving the world that God loves.

Necessary Steps

We live in a post-Christian, restricted nation. The New England church standing tall and white, on the common green in the town square is not the church today. There are restrictions now on what Christians can and can't do in our pluralistic society. While some spend their time fighting that reality (the culture war), others are learning to work within the situation to advance the kingdom. They admit the culture war has been lost, and we must use the tactics of missionaries, using the pathways Christians have been fighting against to our advantage to advance the kingdom.

To transform culture and incarnationally win the lost, *there must be a radical shift from the separatist culture of the 20th century*. In a post-Christian nation, there are several necessary steps. We must shift to a holistic approach that is authentic, relational, multidimensional, caring, dialogical, pre-evangelistic—put simply, a missionary approach.

We must be authentic. This means moving from a church that performs on Sunday to a church that does and is 24/7. Mainstream culture is attracted to things and people who are the same inside as outside. Authenticity must overcome performance.

Relationship is mandatory. We often want people to accept Jesus without dirtying ourselves by becoming friends. As a farmer cannot sow seeds and yield a harvest without his hands in the dirty soil, so we cannot yield a harvest of Spirit fruit without digging our hands into the soil of culture. Friendship evangelism has been proven to be the most effective form of evangelism possible. But friendship demands sacrifice. It takes time, it demands that we learn what they love and what is important to them, and that we listen to their stories. It demands that we laugh and talk about many things before the vulnerable topic of spirituality is even brought up.

To win the lost and transform culture, *we must do away with the strong we/they attitude that comes from a separatist culture*. We must follow our king's incarnational example and establish we/we relationships that lead to love and trust; relationships that allow for the Wholly Gospel to transform lives.

Our relationships must be dialogical. I must not only speak, but I must listen. It may be threatening to hear someone else's ideas, but true relationships are dialogues, not monologues. Our dialogues regarding faith and culture must increasingly use the categories of: bad, good, better, best. A black-and-white conversation does not go far where one worldview is "of the devil" and the other is "of God." Those kinds of labels aren't helpful or friendly. All cultures are centered around religions and philosophies, which have some good in them. I find my discussions go further if I can point out the good of a worldview, then follow up with why I think following Jesus takes that good and goes beyond it to best. Jesus is not threatened by any philosophy or religion. It is often our intimidation and lack of knowledge that wants to label anything else "as the devil." Dialogues that use a model of bad, good, better, best is how most of the world is experienced and allows for dialogues to continue.

Every believer is strategically placed with a unique set of friends, work associates, acquaintances and relatives. *Each of us must work hard to develop our friendships.* If all of our time is absorbed in church functions, this will never happen. We must act as missionaries and give some of our time to building these relationships. In our church, we specifically request that anyone in a community position who comes to faith remain in their position and effectively use it to meet people and transform their sphere of influence.

We must learn to place the accent on pre-evangelism rather than always highlighting evangelism. Pre-evangelism is all the preparation that goes on to prepare a heart to desire Jesus. Paul even said one plants and another waters, but only God makes things grow (1 Corinthians 3:6). Just as a jungle missionary takes time, we must take the time to build relationships, to earn trust and to develop commonality. Those who are traveling the cultural pathways doing this work must be encouraged and held up as models. Too often we shoot at these pioneers and only praise the evangelist who has far less invested.

Our approach must be multidimensional. The church is usually linear in its thinking. We see the space between salvation and transformation like dominos all lined up in row. The first domino for the church is always conversion. The other aspects that need transforming such as marriage, health, or finances, can't be touched until the person converts.

This was not Jesus' approach nor is it the approach of missionaries. We must be multidimensional and bring transformation to whatever area in the person's life it is needed. Perhaps it is their finances or health that needs the touch of Wholly Jesus first. Maybe it is in their marriage. As transformation comes to them in this area of their life, it may also come to their soul. Instead of dominos, it is more like Chinese checkers. There are many marbles moving with different colors all at once. A holistic, multidimensional love for the whole person is what is necessary.

In our community, we are examining the needs of the poor and the suburban poor. The suburban poor have deficits in marriage communication, child rearing and finances. We have begun offering one evening seminars to the community called "In the Living Room" held in neutral venues, inviting neighbors to attend. There is no evangelism but a lot of truth and love. It is a smash success and other churches are joining us.

This approach is a hot button for the cultural fundamentalist, because they fear we will simply do the "social gospel" and never bring the person to a point of conversion. But we must look beyond the Liberals of the early 20th century to the Evangelicals of the 19th century. They practiced and were successful in using this approach without compromising their faith whatsoever.

We must simply become caring. This is ironic to even mention, but it is necessary. Mainstream culture understands compassion. It speaks to them. When the church speaks the gospel without acts of compassion, mainstream culture is distrustful. The church must learn to always incorporate a compassion component in whatever she is doing, whether it's an evangelistic outreach or a Vacation Bible School week for children. Giving ourselves to others is always what we must do: it is the nature of God and we are his image on earth.

We must serve a good cup of coffee. Charlie Peacock, author, artist and producer of several Switchfoot albums, once spoke about the need for believers to learn to do things well. He reminisced about the days of coffee houses when believers were serving decent music and bad coffee. He suggested that as we enter the streams of culture, we learn to do it well. It is only in this way that we gain credibility; that we gain a voice. Whether it is business, the arts, sports, media, politics, education or health, we must learn to serve a good cup of coffee.

In America, we must also humble ourselves and learn from churches in other nations that have been doing this for a long time in restricted cultures. The church in communist, Hindu, Buddhist and Muslim countries has modeled for us what is needed to affect change in America. We need only cast off our high value of saving our own lives for the sake of saving others.

A NEW DAY

We are on the crest of once again seeing evangelical Christianity transforming souls and cultures. The cry of the 19th-century British social reformers, such as William Wilberforce, is being heard. Everywhere I look, believers are stepping out of the church to touch the hurtful, dark parts of culture with the hands of Wholly Jesus. But we must beware that we not repeat the mistakes of the past.

I am grateful for the partners our church has developed in restricted countries around the world. While they have looked to us for assistance, they have taught me a new way to be a pastor in America. I have taken their pre-evangelistic, transformational methods used in restricted countries where direct evangelism is disallowed and applied those concepts here. In countries where the church can't *speak* the Gospel publicly, they *do* the Gospel and their doing is transformational.

Rose Martinez left San Diego just out of college to move to Buddhist Thailand. After almost dying on the streets, she learned the language and started taking in orphans who were being taken or sold into human trafficking. Now after 30 years of labor in Thailand, Burma and Cambodia, and establishing five orphanages, she has earned "merit" in the eyes of her Buddhist contacts by traveling the cultural roads of compassion, health and education. She has brought over Americans to not only work in the orphanages but to teach English in public adult education at the request of a Thai senator.

Even the Buddhist monks respect her and her message.

Sudar and Surita Tappa have labored in Hindu Nepal throughout the last volatile 30 years. Besides planting and pasturing a church in Katmandu, they have orphanages, a home for the elderly, and a Bible School that sends out church planters throughout the country. They have skillfully in prayer worked with and around the repressive government and the rebel Maoists, while being persecuted and occasionally killed by reactionary Hindus. Still, they boldly travel on the pathways of education, government, and medicine, caring for the sick and the elderly, without backing down from church planting in rural parts of the Himalayas.

Their counterpart, Shayam, uses the pathway of sports throughout the Himalayan countries. He and his coaches are able to build trust among families and tribes. Sport is a universal language that allows relationships to develop. Value-based curriculum is also used to transform the character of young athletes. This pre-evangelism sets the stage for the Nepalese to discover a Wholly Jesus they have never known.

Joseph DeSousa has traveled the road of social reform while planting churches throughout India. He has stood as a civil rights leader alongside Dhalit leaders against the repressive Hindu caste system that has allowed the government and businesses to legally enslave people in the dehumanizing work of cleaning gutters and sewers, while raping their women. Their religion and government have protected this abuse for thousands of years.

Now, given another chance by the Dhalits who are quitting Hinduism to escape repression, the Evangelical church is doing the right thing in standing with the poor. As a result, tens of thousands of Dhalits are experiencing a wholly transformation. The holistic Gospel that saves them not only from sin, but also from repression and disease, is being seen and heard and felt.

One lady said to Joseph, "You don't need to preach the message of Jesus to me, you only need to hold my baby and I will believe." These beautiful people only need to see that the church believes in Genesis 1:26, that all people are made in the image of God to be wholly reflections of him. The upper castes can't defile themselves by touching an outcast, but as Christians have stood and eaten with and held the children of Dhalits, they continue to follow Jesus in droves. Christian centers are being built in Dhalit villages that not only function as churches, but also as schools, community and medical centers. Wholly Jesus is known has a holistic savior there. He restores mind, body, spirit and society.

One church in the Arab world travels on many cultural roads, loving their Muslim neighbors with the love of Isa (Jesus). Using sports, medicine, therapy and social work, the church has now grown to into the thousands without ever publicly preaching. Jesus does the preaching in dreams and visions while the church carries out his love in tangible ways every day. Their sports ministry to children brings children of other backgrounds into a value-based curriculum where they play, learn and build relationships with believers. This has become a model in over 200 nations and is even beginning to appear in the U.S., replacing the too often ingrown VBS program. In Madagascar these games have grown to include over 200,000 children in just a few years.

Outside of Cape Town, South Africa, Cassie and Jenny Carstens took a stand against Apartheid as a young pastoral couple within the Dutch Reform Church by working in and sending their daughter to a township school. Now, a trade and computer school has been built to train the people of the township, feed the children a solid meal once a day, and host after school classes. Cassie and Jenny work with the pastors and their wives as equals to strengthen local leadership, marriages and the church in the township. Cassie is also a leader in the transformation movement in Africa, bringing hundreds of thousands of believers together to pray for their continent.

In America, we are moving in the same direction. We are perhaps learning from our foreign brothers and sisters, as they have much to teach us. The disciples of Wholly Jesus involved in magazines, movies, businesses, music, education and politics are choosing to not establish "Christian" projects, but instead are traveling the already established pathways of culture, bringing transformation and a good cup of coffee. Transformation is happening in America like never before. God's kingdom is coming more than we know.

SLEEPING CELLS OF TRANSFORMATION

Karl Marx was right and wrong. If religion is used to separate and quiet the church from mainstream society, it is the opiate of the people. But if it inspires, emboldens and strengthens believers to be like Jesus traveling the pathways of culture, it is the most radical and transforming faith and philosophy the world has ever known.

Al Qaeda has used parts of culture to advance the cause of radical Islam but it is even more marginalized than cultural fundamentalism. But by establishing sleeping cells around the Western world, it is attempting to transform the world through acts of terrorism. Jesus has sleeping churches around the country and world. If ever awakened, these churches would be such a significant transformational force of love that it would usher in the 3rd Great Awakening.

Our creativity, love and courage are needed among believers in every culture and must be matched with the cessation of friendly fire. We must stop attacking believers who reach out to tax collectors and sinners differently that we would. There is no comfort for the church to find itself surrounded by Pharisees and scribes. We must take the risk the first missionary, Jesus, took and reach each subculture inside its own culture with wholly love. We must major on the majors and simultaneously give each other the slack necessary to negotiate the minors as we introduce Jesus to a needy culture.

chapter twelve

Building a Church Without Walls

Love is the movement
Love is a revolution
This is redemption
We don't have to slow back down
— Jon Foreman

O ur minds, like computer screens, bring up an image charged with an emotion when we hear the term "church." The picture in our minds is usually a building. Many have struggled and fought against this phenomenon, insisting that the church is not a building, but people; and that's absolutely true. Unfortunately, it seems that it is impossible to erase 1,600 years of church history. Many idealists curse the day that Constantine made the church legal and buildings started popping up, creating form.

However, my experience tells me that buildings are not the problem. Believers all over the world desire worship/training centers that allow them to move more quickly to advance the kingdom. Unbelievers as well are attracted to centers of worship. There is something very human about wanting a gathering place to worship.

I was so surprised to find this truth on my first trip to Nepal. I spent a day traveling by car and another hiking on foot into the Himalayan foothills, and arrived in a Chapang village untouched by modern civilization. There was no plastic or paper on the ground. There were only huts, chickens and barely clothed believers who wanted to worship and learn about Jesus. But to my idealistic surprise, their hearts' desire was to have a worship/training center, what many call a church. Six thousand dollars was an easy fix for a tin roofed church and they were happy. The problem is not with buildings. The problem is what happens inside and outside church walls.

The other problem regarding church is the emotional charge that people feel when they simply hear that word. For some, it is a nostalgic, cozy feeling that brings back wonderful memories of a New England steeple covered in snow. For others, it is a painful, bitter feeling that reminds them of a religious relationship that went sour. And still for others outside the church, the reactions vary, but many have the picture of an institution that is out of touch with reality, irrelevant, and judgmental. The consequence is that many people today are drawn to Jesus but despise the church.

I remember carrying a heavy Fender Rhodes speaker cabinet into the Unitarian Universalist Congregational Church in Harvard Square, which we rented on Sunday evenings for a church plant. Upstairs another group held a séance, while a third group rented the room next door for a cocktail social hour. We were in the thick of it and I loved it. Every week we hauled our band gear in to worship and study the Bible with largely MIT and Harvard grad students and young business people in the area.

As I was carrying a speaker cabinet in one day I saw a street person passing by the church. Eagerly he asked me what concert was going on inside. I excitedly told him we were having a church meeting and that he was welcome to join us. When he heard the word "church", his face dropped and he responded sternly, "No thanks; I don't do church." So there it is. The church has an image problem. But it also has a purpose problem.

THE CHURCH IN ACTS

The "church" in the Book of Acts was a people in motion, not merely a place to worship. They knew their master's call to be the salt and light of the world. They had been handed the baton by Jesus and now knew they were to run the race. They were the living expression of the body of Wholly Jesus on earth. They were trying to be *a* church when they were gathered for worship and when they were scattered at work and play. They viewed themselves as a transformational kingdom force inward to their community and outward to the world.

When they were gathered, whether in homes or in the temple in Jerusalem, they gathered to worship, study, encourage and love each other, and pray (Acts 2:42). The gathering was not a show, nor was the spotlight on the pastor. Jesus was the focus, and all the believers were ministers. They were Spirit-dependent, not man-dependent. They knew these gatherings were vital to remain salty and full of light.

But the picture of the church was fuzzy. It was not the crisp, clear picture we imagine today when we go church shopping or church critiquing. There was no platonic ideal in the minds of early believers. Everything was new and embryonic, which kept them effective. They were not looking for or trying to be the church—they *were* the church. They knew who they were called to be and what they were called to do, but they were fuzzy about the form. And it was effective because form followed function.

The early chapters of the book of Acts reveal a church that sometimes gathered in homes, sometimes in the temple. But Luke spends little time describing the form of church homes or temple meetings, the organizational polity of the church, the hierarchy or the church services. He gives some of the substance of their gatherings (2:42-44), he shows how the leadership adapted to the needs of the people and recognized gifting (Acts 6), but the form was entirely secondary to the function. The church was on mission, and it didn't involve bricks and mortar.

We have everything reversed. We treat the church like a country club, a restaurant or a theatre. We not only focus on the form, we are absorbed in it. Like neighborhood boys building a tree house, church planters tinker obsessively over creating the perfect form complete with the best bylaws, philosophy, bulletin and logo. Once birthed, this obsession with form becomes the DNA of the church—the church members maintain the focus and invite others to come and see the form. I know of a church with well-defined form that still has no mission to the world 30 years after the successive church plant.

House churches can be just as guilty—most believe their form is the right form. But the house church movement is a form reacting to another form. In reality, there is no right form, only a right function— a right mission.

Church growth seminars have often served recipes for success, but again the focus is on form. Form (style of leadership, music, building, polity, etc) is easily measurable, so the sociology of the church growth movement focuses on what is tangible. Pastors travel to successful churches to learn the secret form. Often they return home, implement the secret form but still see no growth, no success.

Form must follow function. Readers of the book of Acts can make a hermeneutical decision about the form and methods used by the Jerusalem church and later by Paul as he brought the gospel to the Gentiles. We must decide whether to mimic the form and method used by the Jerusalem church or contextualize their reliance on the Spirit for our setting in life. What is clear about all the early churches is their reliance on the Spirit. It is the Spirit and purpose that is emphasized—the form of the church and leadership varies from culture to culture.

If it is the form that matters most then the church will continue to debate between presbyterian, episcopal and congregational polity, between house churches and public buildings, between charismatic and liturgical worship, between one pastor or many pastors ... and the function will not be as effective. Form is not the silver bullet.

When function is in the lead, the form adapts to follow. In an authoritarian culture, an episcopal form of governance may be best. In an exuberant culture, charismatic worship may be best. In an urban location, a club or bar may be the best form for Sunday morning worship.

This is at times difficult for a Western culture to swallow—a culture that is used to the white-steepled church in the town square. But to a culture with an underground or restricted Gospel, the church must adapt to its surroundings. It must keep the main thing the main thing. The where, the how, the who and the when should always follow the why and the what.

The diagram on the following page helps us differentiate between the form of an ineffective church with impermeable walls and an effective church with permeable walls.

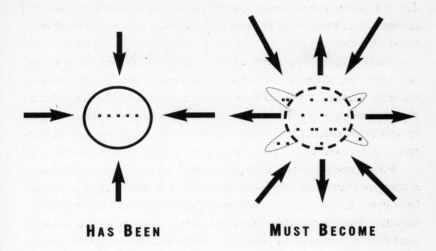

| HAS BEEN | MUST BECOME |

The form on the left is the typical church in the West with defined walls. The direction of movement is entirely inward—the church inviting the community to come to the show and become a part of the club. The form to the right has undefined walls and a freedom of inward and outward movement. The community can freely come in and church members are encouraged to go out into the community.

The small dots represent cell or small group gatherings. On the left the groups are homogonous, well organized and intended to be a smaller, relational repeat of the greater well defined circle. They are designed to keep people in. The cells on the right are heterogeneous, existing in and outside the walls of the church. Their members may be from the church, other churches or community. These cells can be inward *and* outward focused.

LOCKER ROOM OR GAME DAY

Jesus said, "I will build my church, and the gates of hell shall not prevail against it" (Matthew 16:18, KJV). What a powerful image of the church marching against the locked and bolted castle gates of hell, crashing the gates like a battering ram. Jesus imagined the church as a force with which to be contended, by demons and death itself.

But that is not always the picture we have of the church today. Instead, the church is often defensive and hidden like a secluded castle with the drawbridge up and the gates locked. We've figured out how to excel at getting people to the castle, but the force within the castle remains inside the castle walls. The ones we perceive to have this battering ram today are the purveyors of pop culture and subculture. Is the church on the defense or offense? According to Jesus, we must be on the offense. If we are not, our confusion is a problem of purpose.

When we as believers "go to church" whether it is a 5,000-seat auditorium, a quaint tutor chapel with 20 wooden pews or a friend's house with couches, chairs and beanbags, most Christians think of the gathering as the game day. This is the event of the week. This is where we meet God, meet our believing friends and do the great spiritual work. To most people, Sunday morning is game day.

This "game-day" mindset has been magnified by the leaders who recruit us to usher, greet, help in the nursery or teach in children's ministry. This is my assignment. This is what I do on game day. We all play our needful positions with excellence for 90 minutes. The game is lost or won in that time. And when the game is over we go home.

This thinking has been reinforced for hundreds of years. The Puritans, Quakers and prairie Methodists spent their entire Sunday together, with Sunday morning and evening services and a common meal in between. Throughout the Middle Ages, the Cathedrals were packed on Sunday with peasants who had traveled long distances to be with God. Other religions treat their special day as game day as well. The Hindus gather, wash, worship and sacrifice on Saturday. Muslims all over the world worship together on Friday. And for Christians, Sunday morning (or Saturday night) is game day.

Once the game is over, like spent athletes, we return to our homes for a celebratory feast and then a nap, some couch quarterbacking or a trip to the beach. We return to normal again. We worshiped well; we gave our tithe; we taught; we ushered and directed traffic; we served the children and our neighbor in the seat next to us; we took it all in, prayed hard and gave it our best. We represented the team well. Then comes 1:00 PM Sunday; the game is over and we can come down. We'll do our best to follow Jesus during the week and then comes Saturday night, and we prepare again for game day.

Pastors especially have this mindset. Sunday is show time. It is where the great message is preached, the great funds are collected, the great songs are sung and the great services are proffered. Success is won or lost by increased attendance, bigger offerings, better teachings, a worshipful experience and/or excellent environments. The novice quickly learns that this event, above all else, is important. Sunday is game day.

I have no intent to diminish the importance of believers gathering together. It is crucial. I only want to challenge the assumed purpose and measures of success, and then I want to change the metaphor.

The gathering is not the game. It is merely the locker room pep talk. It is where we worship Jesus in song, where diagrams are drawn out on the chalkboard so that we can see what's working and what isn't. It is a time for our coaches to encourage us to play our positions with excellence outside the walls, on the green fields of culture. After our locker room talk, we then play the game throughout the week. Come the next Sunday, we celebrate, encourage each other and again prepare for the next game, the next week.

I know my metaphor will offend some. Locker rooms are not always pretty. Some will argue that worship is important to declare God's worth and to invoke his presence, and I will agree. They will assert that Jesus is somehow mysteriously present as we gather, especially at the Lord's supper, and I will agree. They will say that together with the Reformers, the preaching of God's Word transforms lives, and I will agree. That prayer in itself is vital and changes things, and I will agree. But I will also insist that the church on earth has not fulfilled its purpose until it returns to the streets. The game is played there, not within the walls of the church.

When what goes on inside the walls is treated as the game, an unfortunate thing happens. Each worshipper checks a box in their mind that says, "I played well." Like a worshipper climbing Mount Zion, we have reached the peak.

But when the church service becomes the locker room, a different mindset occurs. We emerge into mainstream life anticipating the game, playing the game and ultimately winning the game. We work and serve throughout the week as living sacrifices, following and obeying Jesus in our day-to-day lives. Our weekdays become the worship service.

If this weren't the case, whenever a believer accepts Jesus they might as well be immediately beamed into heaven. If church is only about Sunday, what good is the week?

Pastors and leaders must take on the mindset of coaches. They are not the players or performers. We don't applaud their performance on Sunday; we let them prepare us for our performance on Monday through Saturday. We have a mission to fulfill, a game plan to employ, and we all have strategic roles to play. We must play them well, and give all we are capable of giving.

THE RETREAT BEHIND THE WALLS

There is a regressive nature to the church. Without a concerted effort on the part of the leadership and members, the walls of the church will become so high and thick that the church will quickly lose its cultural influence entirely. The leadership must fight hard to create permeable walls that allow the believers to come in, be trained and be filled with the Spirit so that they can go out into society and reflect Wholly Jesus well.

The "kingdom of self" exists corporately as well as individually. It is so easy to be caught up in ourselves, and what we do for ourselves, that we forget about other churches and the community at large. Unchanged, the outward momentum of God's kingdom is at risk of being lost. The Western church will become the means and the end in itself.

Yes, the church needs to be a sacred place for people to worship, a locker room where we can learn, train and be encouraged by each other. But at the end of the day, the church must prepare followers of Jesus to go out and not get comfortable staying in. Each church must remember that it is part of a bigger plan than its own. We are not the kingdom of God but the king is urging us outward to proclaim and advance the kingdom.

Obviously there are exceptions. New believers with a history of addiction or crime will often do best to withdraw into the sanctuary of the church for a season—perhaps we might say these are followers on injured reserve, spending a short season in recovery and rehabilitation before venturing back onto the field.

However, for most us who come to faith in Jesus, our day-to-day environment is our playing field and our friends, co-workers, family and colleagues are future disciples. The people in our sphere of influence are not the competition on the field, but rather the fans watching the game. What they see us do tangibly on the field impacts them. We might even bring them on the field with us so they can experience the kingdom work firsthand—so they can see the image of God reflected on our faces up close.

Believers must be encouraged to continue in their relationships. Paul reminded the Corinthians that our separatism was never intended toward the mainstream culture: In 1 Corinthians 5:9-11, he says, *I have written you in my letter not to associate with sexually immoral people—not at all meaning the people of this world who are immoral, or the greedy and swindlers, or idolaters. In that case you would have to leave this world.* Soccer coaches, business professionals, artists, corporate leaders and PTA volunteers must continue in their relationships if the church is to find traction in society. The reverse model, "redemption and lift," where the believer drops every involvement to only participate in church activities is an ineffective model.

The point here is simple: without a concerted effort on the part of leadership, the church will become ingrown, a narcissistic institution that has lost its purpose. The walls will grow higher and thicker as better programs and cooler environments are available for church members. Volunteerism within the church will become so demanding that Christian involvement in the community is lost. We can become a parallel universe to society outside: a separate culture with separate friends and separate events. We can withdraw from society and from other churches.

We must not let the walls define us. Our purpose is that of salt and light. We are a transforming agent to our surroundings and we cannot transform from inside the walls of the church.

I once visited a gathering of 60 people piled in a living room hoping to become a church. I asked the group, "How many were have been hanging around unbelievers?" They all shook their heads. Then I responded, "You've lost your purpose." We must move the church closer to the community and the community closer to the church. How do we do this?

BUILDING A CHURCH WITHOUT WALLS

Like the membrane of human cells, the church must develop permeable walls. Thankfully, the membranes of biological cells are impermeable to many harmful substances. In the same way, the church has learned to be guarded against false doctrine and sinful behavior. But it is not so sophisticated when it comes to protecting against values and behavior that are counterproductive to the kingdom. Nor is the church always wise to discern between the major and minor doctrines of scripture. It is important for each church to have its own beliefs, but if it has no sense of minors and majors, it will never fellowship with other churches. To have permeable walls and exist as a transforming agent in culture, a church must become wise to these issues.

With human cells, it is not only important that the walls guard against unwanted molecules, it is equally important that the proper molecules be allowed to travel in and out through the permeable walls. Likewise the church must become sophisticated in allowing unbelievers to come into the church without compromising the integrity of the organism. Equally, it must be strategic in encouraging the members to travel through the membrane into mainstream life. For all of this to happen it must become quite intentional in its nucleus: its purpose, beliefs, values and practices. If the nucleus is too undefined and weak, it will overreact and protect itself by forming impermeable walls, keeping believers in and unbelievers out.

Walls from the very beginning were used to keep people in and out. They were built for protection. Jericho, one of the oldest cities known to archeology, is also the oldest fortified city known to antiquity, protecting itself from armies and marauding nomads. At night the city gates were always closed.

But for a fortified desert city to survive, it had to allow commerce during the day. Although guards were posted at the gates, goods and food could travel in and out to keep the city both safe and thriving. But in the end, no wall could keep this great city safe from the kingdom of God. He brought down the walls of Jericho with a corporate shout.

Many have gone on prayer walks around cities and to different countries, asking God to bring down the walls of the city to let in the kingdom of God. It is time that we also pray that the walls of the church come down, allowing the kingdom to go out and penetrate culture.

A church must decide its purpose. Some pastors like long theological explanations of the church, which often include the shorter Westminster confession: to glorify God and enjoy him forever. But we must all ultimately answer the question: how does the church glorify God on this planet? Whether the metaphors of salt and light are used or the picture of fruit, ultimately the church is to be the most powerful transformation force in society.

When a newcomer does visit the church, the walls must be permeable enough that the visitor feels loved, welcomed and accepted. The visitor must not feel he is culturally awkward or weird. The barriers must not be cultural, but spiritual. The cross and resurrection event is ultimately the only barrier a newcomer must face.

This is a challenge because the church often wants to voice its opinion on some social or political zeitgeist. For certain, the church needs to be aware and involved in these cultural matters, but if the involvement is carried out in a harsh, derogatory manner, a we-are-better-than-they-are message is communicated. Visitors needing a touch from Wholly Jesus will receive only a socio-political barrage of words. They often won't return for more of something they can find in abundance on talk radio and the internet.

To use the issue of abortion or sexual preference as an example, the church has for a generation taken strong and vocal stances on these subjects. The church needs to be a prophetic voice to society and particularly in a democracy where we have a say in the direction of law. But *how* it is done is as important as *what* is said. The method is as much the message as the message itself.

In most church services, there are those who have had abortions and have experimented with or have been aware of homosexual tendencies. Any teaching, announcement or petitions must keep that in mind. Like a surgeon performing a delicate procedure, the words must communicate love and acceptance for all. The old adage, "love the sinner and hate the sin", must be lived out and certain sins must not be picked on more than others. All sin is sin.

I was once misunderstood and accused of not being forthright enough when I disallowed anti-abortion petitioners to greet our worshippers with the request for their signature as they entered the auditorium. I insisted the petitioners retreat to the booth they had been given so that people could approach them freely. I insisted that our church remain a safe place where anyone could come in, regardless of their past, their beliefs and their political orientation and experience the love of Jesus. Obviously, the church needs to be clear and teach on various moral subjects. But it also needs to be a safe, investigative place where the visitor is not clobbered over the head with everything we believe. The church ought to enter relationships as any healthy individual would. In most healthy relationships, commonality and friendship precede confrontation.

Further, where we are roaring lambs about certain social issues, we must learn to be aware of all the issues and roar faithfully about all issues. The suburban church has typically roared about the issues that threaten our suburbs: drugs, homosexuality and abortion, yet it has remained curiously silent on other issues such as social injustice, crime and ecology. The urban church roars about poverty, civil rights, crime and social injustice, but it is often quiet on issues of sexual preference and the value of the unborn. We cannot be selfishly selective about our causes. We must roar consistently otherwise we appear to be merely elephants or donkeys, not roaring lambs who follow radical Jesus.

Making a church accessible to the community is the easier part of the equation. An accessible worship service with friendly greeters and easy to follow announcements can make any visitor feel welcome. But releasing the members of the church to go outside the walls into the community is the more difficult part of the equation and here's why. Every church needs each member's volunteer time, energy and money. If the members are released, the economic foundation of the church is at risk. There is the genuine possibility that church members may become engrossed in their community and less available to the church. They may even lose their purpose and become caught up in a dangerous cultural current. But these are risks we, the church, must take—and our leaders must encourage us to take. We must see that the player on the bench is not at risk for injury—only apathy and atrophy. The players on the field are at risk for injuries small to severe—even death. They risk much more than those on the bench, but they are also the ones who win and have full rights to celebration and reward.

A tangible example is actually from the world of sports. Our culture has a very sophisticated network in the world of sports. It is a wonderful opportunity for the missional believer. But Christians who begin to participate in sports are drawn away from spending time in the church. As they move from recreational play to serious travel teams, the commitment level increases. The tension often becomes so intense that the church demands the player become more serious about church and reduce his or her level of involvement in sports. "You must choose between youth group and sports."

But a church without walls encourages athletes to travel the cultural pathway and travel with them. The permeable walls adapt to the opportunity and trains athletes how to live for Christ on the field. The church reduces the tension by adapting and encouraging athletes rather than lifting them from their passion.

This example is transferable to all the pathways of culture: music, business, technology, health care, etc. Christians have no problem loving Jesus; they just don't know what to do with their lives. The church's role is not to hinder them from living but to train and release them to be fully human and to holistically walk with Christ in their sphere of influence. Our form of church must not hinder the advancement of the kingdom of God. As followers of Christ, we must adapt to the leading of Christ.

WALLS BETWEEN CHURCHES

Most churches are not against each other, the pastors are just too busy trying to keep their own castle stable. Unity for them is simply not being against each other.

But there is a strong argument for raising the bar of unity to actually doing ministry together. United prayer and ministry within or outside the church is an important display not only to the world (John 17), but also to ourselves. We need each other.

Years ago a pastor friend of mine from the next town over took a team to Hungary. The following year, he didn't have the funds to go. Another church volunteered to fund the trip. My friend was so surprised and asked, "Why are you doing this?" The other pastor responded, "Because you're me. If you are blessed, I am blessed. We wear the same jersey."

In the northern coastal part of San Diego where I live, 60 local pastors gather together for monthly prayer and a quarterly training lunch. There, relationships are born and continue to grow. The original thinking was that one pastor alone influences on average maybe 300 people. But collectively we influence all the churches, perhaps 20,000 or more people. If pastors everywhere will work together in this way, training, praying for and assisting each other, they can influence a much greater number of people without adding staff, budget or buildings. They increase their sphere of influence.

Where other churches are concerned, the church must move from a competition model to a cooperation model, understanding we all wear the same uniform. As local churches and parachurches work together, the community is transformed faster and more effectively. Where one succeeds, we all succeed—and the kingdom is advanced.

A NEW WAY TO BE THE CHURCH

The church is not the kingdom of God (the rule and reign of God on earth) but it is designed to be a carrier of the kingdom. It recognizes that the world (*the cosmos*), or the kingdom of darkness, is the illegitimate occupying force that overlays our world. Like a cloud, it permeates the values and conduct of the citizens of this world. It often thickly resides in forms called churches.

But citizens of the kingdom of heaven are here not to offer church, but to offer his salt and light into every individual and corporate sphere of influence. We have experienced Wholly Jesus and we are now his messengers of wholeness to this world. We are thus the primary force that opposes the kingdom of darkness—we are the force that will ultimately bring about its destruction. When our movement—the church's movement—is outward, there is to be no place on this planet that is too far, too low or too dark for the truth and love of Jesus. Gathered in worship, we must teach, train, pray, encourage and love one another for the purpose of empowering us to fulfill our mission.

We understand that we don't worship a localized deity. God is omnipresent and, in that sense, "This is my Father's world." Therefore, we walk in the Spirit, in our sphere of influence, down cultural pathways to transform this world with Jesus' love. Sometimes people surrender to Jesus first before anything else is transformed. Other times we heal, counsel, feed, vote, visit or console before a person surrenders their soul. Each of us understands that we are the hands and feet of Wholly Jesus on earth. In a multidimensional, multicultural way, we go out, we reach out. Our church leadership and form must not only accommodate this calling, it must enforce it.

For Wholly Jesus to permeate Western culture, the church must not only travel the pathways on which culture already exists, but it must also befriend the people along those pathways. There is no question that friendship evangelism is the most effective form and this requires authentic, not synthetic friendships. In that context, the incarnate context of relationships, we must allow our actions and our words to reflect the nature of Jesus, the image of God. We must be ourselves in every way God intends.

In this way, the church is without walls. The walls exist only to define the uniqueness of that individual church (location, leadership, doctrinal and value emphasis and commitment), but they remain permeable to allow and encourage people to come in and go out.

The leadership must relinquish its control and fear of releasing the people. It must move from a *transactional* model where the people worship and give, and the pastor in turn gives them a sermon, to a *transformational* model where the people are there to be transformed so they might go out and transform their world.

We must especially invest in the transformation of children and youth since they are the future church. We must stop merely entertaining them and begin training and initiating them into their mission. We must teach them at an early age that Bible study, prayer, worship, giving and fellowship are vital to their survival. We must teach them to be intentional invaders, making lists of people they are praying for and befriending. They must experience community projects designed to transform schools, neighborhoods and cities. They must learn to obey the nudges of the Spirit as we follow this radical Wholly Jesus. And they must know the loudest form of evangelism is always love.

Our leaders must lead. We must stop obsessing over form, imagining that one day we will find the silver bullet to a successful church. We must get on with the business we have been called to conduct. Church size, polity, style and building must follow function. Every facet of the ministry must have an outward component.

On our staff we ask all of our pastors and directors to have at least one of their goals be the mobilization of people outward toward the community. Home groups have taken on homeless teenagers and building homes in Mexico. Our cultural apologetics pastor now hosts an art exhibit for the community. Our youth have developed their own missions budget reaching into the barrio. Our marriage and family department now offers marriage and family seminars for the community in a non-religious community center. Our women's ministry works with women in Nicaragua, Thailand and South Africa to promote their handmade jewelry and clothing in the States and then sends the profits back to the local women. Our people feel free to write for mainstream magazines, create culturally significant movies and music, build homes, teach in public schools and govern our cities with the fragrance of Christ.

Like Nehemiah, ignoring the threats of Sanballat and Tobiah, we leaders must learn to ignore those who want to simply live on the defensive and judge others' efforts—those who shoot at others first and ask questions later. There will always be separatists who would circle the wagons out of fear to protect us from the strange people we have been called to reach. But we must follow our incarnate God into the world. When Chuck Smith began to reach long-haired hippies for Christ there was plenty of criticism to throw around. There were plenty of Sanballats and Tobiahs around to criticize his efforts. He didn't require them to cut their hair, change their apparel or stop playing rock music.

Leaders must be strategic. Scan the community for the physical, emotional, relational and spiritual needs that exist. Scan internally to assess your resources. Then prioritize the projects that the church will corporately adopt since all the needs cannot be addressed at once or even in one year. Decide whether each project is to be done by the whole church, one small group in the church or if it is an interchurch project. Pray to develop a strategy. Encourage the staff to increasingly focus their budget outwardly. Become aware of organizations who already are doing kingdom work in the community. Partner wherever possible with other organizations, churches or community groups.

The Fellowship of the Ring was a wonderful example of the church. The strange unity between a dwarf, an elf, a wizard, men and hobbits was only possible through the higher intention of the mission—to toss the evil ring into the volcanic soup of Mordor. As they were on the journey, a strange love began to develop for one another despite their different gifts, personalities and abilities. It was only when the individuals began thinking of themselves that the strange band of travelers began to fall apart. As they lost their outward calling, their fellowship imploded.

The love, unity and resulting form of the church is only found and kept while we maintain our common outward momentum to be salt and light.

chapter thirteen

Wholeness Will Prevail

All the darkness in the world cannot extinguish the light of a single candle.

— St. Francis of Assisi

After a brief walk on the beach, I have once again washed ashore at Swami's Café, across the street from the Self Realization Fellowship. I notice there are a few more additions to the bulletin board:

Wisdom Healing Qigong with Master Gu—Inner Medicine

Now to Wow—physical coaching

REIKI CLASSES—UNIVERSAL LIFE HEALING

Cre8wellness—what to eat and why

I enjoy the usual Acai berry bowl and a Swiss cheese omelet with Italian chicken sausage. And now, savoring a mug of dark roasted Guatemalan coffee, I'm ready to write again. But before beginning, I ponder once more the fact that no offering of Wholly Jesus can be found on the bulletin board of wholeness.

IT IS CRITICAL THAT JESUS ENTER THE CONVERSATION

While walking the beach recently, I ran into a friend who poured his heart out to me regarding his suicidal daughter. His daughter, Christy, was raised in the church, attended a local junior high youth group and has heard about Jesus all her life. But after making a commitment as a child, she is now an unbelieving college student. Here's why:

Christy grew up in a global, pluralistic, holistic, ecological society for which she was told, "Jesus didn't care." Her youth pastor told her that Jesus didn't care about world peace, only the apocalypse. He didn't care about the wellness of the body, only the soul. He didn't care about the people of other faiths, only Christians. He didn't care about art and culture. He didn't care about ecology; the planet was going to burn anyway. And he didn't care about the integration of science and her faith. And the reason she could be sure Jesus didn't care about these things is because none of these things were mentioned in the Bible. Jesus just wanted her to pray, read her Bible and tell others about him. But eventually the tension between the real world and this fabricated youth-pastor's world snapped. In order to be true to herself and her passion about these issues, she had to abandon the otherworldly Jesus she'd known. Christy is an example of tens of thousands of Christians who have learned to disassociate a thin Jesus from their own wellbeing, along with the wellbeing of society and the planet.

Even now that she is suicidal and struggling with clinical depression, Christy won't turn to Jesus because she believes he doesn't care. In fact, some believers have frowned on the fact that she is seeing a psychiatrist and taking medication. Mainstream society must think we believers are crazy at times.

Is that what we deduce from Scripture simply because Jesus "never mentions" nutrition, ecology, globalization or pluralism? Jesus doesn't mention cars, light bulbs, toilets, burritos or televisions, but Western Christians seem to have no problem using these and incorporating them into their lifestyles. Wise believers learn to think Christianly and apply Jesus' teachings to all areas of their lives. If a separatist church continues this disconnect with mainstream culture, we risk losing an entire generation. Does Jesus only care about sin, souls and heaven? Where is the bold, in the midst-of-culture, healing-the-sick, feeding-the-poor Jesus of the Gospels?

Missionaries, starting with the Apostle Paul on Mars Hill, have understood the importance of penetrating culture and adapting our approach contextually to effectively present Christ to society. "I have become all things to all men so that by all possible means I might save some" (1 Corinthians 9:22). Just as the apostle Paul adapted his message to the context of Athens, missionaries since Hudson Taylor have used a holistic approach, contextualizing their approach to the respective countries. Now these missionary voices cry out to the Western church to become more missional to its own surrounding lands, and come out of its safe castles.

We must turn from our separatist stance *against* culture to an approach of *penetrating* culture. It is time for the church to broaden its reactionary, narrow, soul-only religion to a robust evangelical faith for the whole person. America longs for the pulpit and the pew to teach and model the redemption of all things. But this world and culture are moving fast and will not wait for the church.

What Makes Wholeness So Difficult?

The Africans tell us that large, difficult issues are like eating an elephant. It has to be eaten one bite at a time. The subject of wholeness is an elephant, no question. It is a difficult and complex subject for many reasons.

For one, our *brokenness* as a human race is so complex and expansive. We are interpersonally, biologically, intrapersonally, socially, psychologically and spiritually broken. In fact, it's easy to be overwhelmed with the enormity of our human condition. Therefore, we cringe at and distrust any simplistic, cure-all people, products or therapeutic techniques that don't do justice to the complex situation. But the world awaits an intelligent, redemptive, Christian response. They wait for the offering of Wholly Jesus.

Wholeness is further complicated by the fact that *Eastern religions dominate* the wholeness conversation. Christians have thus been reticent to enter the dialogue on wholeness. Perhaps, fearing compromise or condemnation of the church, we have allowed the Eastern religions to be the prevailing influence.

Another complicating issue is the fear that churches and holistic believers will become imbalanced and *leave the centrality of Jesus.* It's a fear that we will be branded the "therapeutic, meditation, recovery, homeless, political, ecological church" and accused of abandoning the simplicity of bringing people into relationship with Wholly Jesus. To enter this culture or any culture there is always a risk of being conformed by the culture and being misunderstood by the separatists. But to play it safe and not climb Mars Hill is to give this world away to others.

Perhaps the biggest barrier is the 20th century church's emphasis on the *immaterial world.* There are some primary reasons for this: 1) Inconsistent success in the physical and social realm has encouraged the church to bank on the unseen rather than the seen. 2) The division between the liberals and the fundamentalists of the early 20th century has led the conservative branch of the church to abdicate their own 19th century emphasis on social reform. 3) The influence of Western, Platonic thinking continues to hamper the church. 4) The perceived delay of the second coming of Jesus has caused much of the church to postpone any expected physical or social salvation until his return. These ingredients have created an ironic dualistic, inconsistent church where members privately enjoy and protect their physical belongings, corporately build physical buildings, but sing songs and teach about the immaterial.

I have suggested that an already-but-not-yet approach to the kingdom of God is a better solution than following Plato. In this redemptive approach, Jesus' salvation is partially realized in all of life, and he decides what will be partial (but-not-yet)—we do not. Kingdom believers celebrate the forgiveness of our sins and live an increasingly transformed character. In addition, we pray for the sick, feed the poor, speak out about injustice, protect the planet and promise hope for the future. To do any less is to misrepresent Jesus and presume we control the timing and plan for redemption. I humbly admit that not every earthly problem will be solved, but neither does every-

one I share Jesus with become saved. I don't cease to share, and in the
same way, I shouldn't cease to solve.

In a day when wholeness, ecology, peace and justice are on the
hearts of the world, it is perilous to say that Jesus has nothing to say
until the second coming. This backs the church into a corner it should
not be in. Wholly Jesus is concerned about it all and will put it all
right. There is no question that the wellness of the soul is to be
emphasized and given priority, but salvation in the hands of Wholly
Jesus was, is and always will be seamless. It will reach every part of our
humanity and our world.

To not promote wholeness as Jesus did, is to promote apathy or
indifference at best. This is not a day for ostriches. We must lift our
heads from the sands of our cultural past and dive into the mainstream
conversations on human wholeness. As believers we know too much
to cop out now. We know too much about the problem, too much
about the kingdom message and too much about the social and ecological implications if we fail to act and speak out now. Most of all, we
know too much about the heart of Jesus. Wholeness is at the core of
the Gospel. It is the evangel that drives us into the conversation. We
must climb Mars Hill and enter the dialogue with our message of
redemption.

A CONTRIBUTION LARGER THAN "CHRISTIAN"

Before my sons were signed to their first label we had a discussion
about "Christian" music. We were driving together down the freeway
and the question of the hour was "Are you a Christian band?" Just
then a car drove by with a fish on the rear window. I asked, "Is that a
Christian car?" The point was simple. Objects can't be labeled
"Christian," only people. We mistakenly think everything that has the
label "Christian" stuck to it is redeemed.

"Christian" is used often as an adjective by both believers and
mainstream culture, but the meaning and the emotional charge,
whether positive or negative, vary. Originally in the New Testament,
it was used strictly as a noun, describing Christ's followers (Acts
11:26). Now, it is used to describe everything from music and books

to professionals and businesses. Anything done by a believer may be called "Christian." But we are often naïve regarding its impact and meaning in culture. We must learn to be wise about using the term as an adjective. What we think is advancing the cause may in fact be hindering the advancement of the kingdom in our sphere of influence.

Some believers use the term as if it is synonymous with "safe." I need to get my son or daughter into a Christian school, listening to Christian music, seeing a Christian therapist. Others seem to mean the person or product is "good or reliable." And others are just distinguishing the product or industry from secular or mainstream culture.

But we must be aware that although the label "Christian" may seem useful, it also carries with it some problems. It alienates some, it sets up a false expectation for others, and sometimes it is misleading. It may also offer a veneer redemption.

As missional believers, we must learn that the overuse of the term "Christian" creates and maintains a we/they world, which widens the moat between the castle church and the culture outside its walls. It alerts the mainstream world that this product or person is someone to avoid. If we will be missionaries to our culture, we must be careful about we/they language and strive for we/we opportunities to create friendship that leads to an ongoing dialogue.

We must learn from our brothers and sisters in restricted countries who have no industry (books, music or movies) that are Christian. They have no "Christian" baristas, accountants or mechanics. They only have believers who do an excellent job and build relationships and promote truth without waving the adjective. As the church moves beyond Christ against culture to Christ penetrating culture our strategies must change.

If something is true, it is true; it is not strictly a Christian truth. If the coffee is good, it's good without it being served in a Christian café. If the music is good, it's good without calling it Christian. I think Bono once expressed his caution about calling U2's music Christian, admitting, "I would not want to blame my music on Christ." Duke Ellington said it best: "There are only two kinds of music: good and bad."

If believers are to follow Jesus into culture we must be leery of the we/they categories. They work wonderfully for a separatist church that wants to put the "safety" label on products to protect its parishioners. But labels make it difficult for those trying to invade and influence culture with the wholly redemption of Wholly Jesus. There is certainly a unique Christian worldview regarding wholeness, but for us to claim aspects of medicine, nutrition and therapy as "Christian" can do far more harm than good. My Arab friends understand this completely as they follow Wholly Jesus into the Muslim world. Why alienate, they say, before the conversation happens? The adjective often ends the conversation, but truth, goodness, beauty and love keep the conversation going.

I know there are industries formed in which it may be useful to distinguish the content of the material, for example, "Christian" books and music. And sometimes without this distinction, the mainstream industry would not publish books or music with such content. So these industries have allowed artists and authors to flourish. Nevertheless, even here the goal of being salt and light in our culture; we can't simply be content to be salt and light to each other. Artists and authors who can make it travel mainstream with their talents must be encouraged to do so.

Ultimately, something is redeemed when it fulfills God's intentions. An object, an industry or a person being redeemed is becoming more and more what God intended. Our contribution to the wholeness movement is therefore much more than simply calling something Christian. Nothing captures this thought of thorough redemption more than the scene in Lewis' *The Magician's Nephew*. The witch, in fear of Aslan, hurls an iron rod torn from a lamppost, and when the rod hits Aslan's head it falls to the ground and grows into a brand new lamppost. Everything must be redeemed and will be by Christ!

THE TRUE UNIQUENESS OF OUR CONTRIBUTION

I'm in the meditation garden again. Once again, my prized bench is taken, this time by a woman on a cell phone. My second favorite holds a man in deep lotus meditation. Jesus belongs here, so I sit nearby and peck away on my laptop.

I know that the wholeness movement—the movement these two are likely engrossed in—is lacking a definition of a complete human being. It is moving headlong toward a wellness without an understanding of the true image of a whole person. I would like to help them see. Perhaps I am the first reflection they have seen.

The secret remedy for wholeness is found in the *image of God*. We, more than anyone, know the purpose and value of a person. But ours is an alien wholeness. Without this understanding, our purely human pursuit of wholeness is a house of smoke and mirrors—we are only reflecting different images of ourselves. God's nature provides us the objective definition and dignity that the wholeness movement needs.

We equally bring the *pneumatic, immaterial aspect* of a whole person to the dialogue. We are not completely unique in this regard, but our theistic understanding of spirituality is distinct. Human wholeness without spiritual wholeness is not thorough. We are spirit beings. The priority of the soul is vital. A quadriplegic that knows her soul is forgiven and a new body awaits her, has discovered an important truth on the path of wholeness. Understanding the already-but-not-yet kingdom of Jesus will encourage the person who is being spiritually transformed but still longs for a transformed body. In this life, mortality is certain, but this does not diminish the importance of the healing and care for the physical body, city and planet. To not do so is to follow Plato not Jesus. Ultimately, we are not merely spirits. In the new heaven and earth, we all get a new body. The Bible knows nothing of an immaterial, spiritual-only salvation. The salvation Wholly Jesus brings will be a thorough bio-psycho-socio-spirito wholeness. All creation groans for this wholeness (Romans 8:19-21).

Believers also uniquely force the conversation to come out of denial regarding the extent of our *brokenness*. When it comes to being honest about the brokenness of people and this planet, believers are not Pollyannas nor are we pessimists. We are realists who believe the planet and the people on it are severely broken. We accept that our fallen mutation is thorough and has affected every part of life. Any wholeness theory or technique that denies brokenness cannot get far. There is no need to minimize the problem to believe in a solution. If I have eight broken bones but the orthopedic doctor treats only two, six will remain broken and will perhaps heal improperly. Our human denial of brokenness keeps us from seeing the urgency and thoroughness of the solution. We must uniquely call society out of denial.

Forgiveness, in the last decade has become a hot research topic for psychological journals, but it has uniquely been the cornerstone of pastoral counseling for centuries. Over 600 refereed journal articles have been written on forgiveness in the last 10 years.[1] Forgiveness given by God is spiritual healing that provides intrapersonal healing, which then allows for interpersonal healing. Repairing the pains of the past and the wounded emotions is vital to the health of a person. Forgiveness is vital to the wellbeing of friendships and nations. Jesus knew the importance of forgiveness and he offered it openly.

A loving, personal relationship with God is the pearl of Biblical wholeness. It is the cure for the longing that drives every man and woman to search for meaning in life. It is this personal relationship in which we are called "friends" of God that profoundly stands out against the pantheistic backdrop of modern holism (John 15:13-14). God is neither energy nor a projection of me. He is not merely an extension of the self; He is the divine Other. This is what we were made for and what we have found in the Wholly Jesus.

Transformation of character and moral behavior is also at the heart of Christian wholeness. Wholeness without moral transformation is nonsensical. The ancients of all religions and philosophies knew that wisdom regarding character and behavior was at the core of human, and in turn societal, wellbeing. How we treat others is germane to the human dilemma. What is unique to Wholly Jesus' offering is how our character is transformed within Christianity. Believers not only believe in forgiveness, but also in moral transformation through the work of the Spirit. Ours is not a try-harder religion, but a response of faith to the cross and resurrection that brings forth an ongoing transformed character and behavior. It is a relational response of "yes" to Jesus' sacrifice for sins, to his physical resurrection of power and new life, to the mystical reality that the sinful part of the believer died with Christ and lives a new life today. And it is a "yes" to his behavioral and character promptings by his Spirit. But the core of this "yes" is a relationship of loyal love. If you've ever been around a new Christian who had some crusty old habits, you can see the tangible effect of this character transformation. Truly a person becomes transformed so much that even his countenance is changed.

Physical wholeness has always been central to Christian wholeness as well. Jesus healed the sick, the early church held the care of people's bodies in high regard and most of Christian history has not promoted a dualism between medical and supernatural healing.[2] All healing is good and comes from God. There has never been a time where some aspect of the church hasn't recognized the importance of the care of the body. Many of the hospitals in this country and around the world were originally built from funds and a theology that came from the influence of Christianity.

Social reform and issues of justice have also long been a part of Wholly Jesus' message—since the time of the Old Testament prophets. God is a just God. This gives meaning to the concept of judgment, forgiveness and the work of the cross. Justice will prevail. God cares deeply about the injustices in the land. The 19th century evangelicals understood this and so must we. The younger generation is flocking to champion the cause of justice in every way imaginable, but they desperately need pastors to guide them.

Care of the planet was the assignment given to the first humans, and it is absolutely a Christian agenda. Green is a Christian color not a liberal color. To be sure methodology greatly complicates the subject of conservation. But Christians must ultimately be true to Scripture not a political party because caring for this planet is a spiritual mandate. Ultimately, politics are downstream from culture and if the church is penetrating culture it is influencing politics—not the other way around. It is time for the church to take the lead.

Equally unique is the *method and style* by which we give the message of Wholly Jesus. It is the least, the last and the children who are first in the kingdom. Our style, like Jesus', is not to harshly yell in the streets and break a bruised reed.[3] Ours is not a mean, darn-right platform, but a quiet and persistent doing. Humility and love form our style, making the message and the method one and the same. Ours is the resting knowledge that Jesus will ultimately redeem all things and the mustard seed will grow into a large tree (Mark 4:31-32).

Also unique is the realistic awareness that we will never complete the task without *Jesus' second coming*. We are not naïve or deluded, thinking we can transform the world without Jesus. We still need the king to come and finish the project. This is not Triumphalism. We are not yet kings and queens reigning without him (1 Corinthians 4:8). We wait for his return to complete the transformation he offers. We truly live in the already-but-not-yet position between the two comings. His first coming culminated with the cross and resurrection, and it is the foundation and power behind personal and social transformation. But it will be Wholly Jesus the king, at his second coming, who will make individuals, society and this planet completely whole.

Platonism and Docetism are not the antidote to Triumphalism. We must both follow Jesus' example in his first coming and usher in his second coming. We must bravely follow and present Jesus and his nature to the real substantive world.

The Gospel message is about a savior who came to save the whole person, the whole human race, on the whole physical planet. This makes us contextual, multidimensional evangelists, bringing wholeness to a person in various ways while always placing their relationship with Jesus in the center. Rather than a linear approach, where we don't feed, help their marriage, bandage their wounds or paint their fences until they accept Jesus, we take a multidimensional approach and allow Wholly Jesus to decide where his transformation work will begin.

We are uniquely missional. Christianity above all faiths believes it has good news to give to the entire world. This belief requires us to penetrate every culture and sub-culture in a relevant manner. Missionally-minded people around the world understand the importance of a holistic, multidimensional approach to salvation and the kingdom. The younger generation "gets it" seamlessly.

In the same way, we must confess that we are not ever completely transformed in this life. We are realists. We are wounded healers who press on with scars that speak volumes to a world that already knows, without the bumper sticker reminding us, that Christians are not perfect.

★★★

Today I visited a friend who is dying. Blaine and his wife Kathy are amazing people who walk close to Jesus and bless all who visit them. But the fact remains that Blaine is dying and has been for years. His aorta is slowing tearing, causing excruciating knife-like pains in his chest. The condition of his heart disallows surgery, so he is in a terminal state. From a wheelchair, he confessed to me, "Little by little you watch as another part of you is taken away."

As I drove away from their mobile home I pondered once again, what is wholeness? Blaine longs to be whole. But with all of us, he awaits his ultimate healing. Wholeness is a holy subject. God is whole. Ours is only the image of God and we are wounded healers, healing and at the same time longing to be more whole.

WHAT IS REQUIRED TO CHANGE THINGS?

Back at Swami's Café, two young ladies sit next to me and ask if I know the location of the meditation gardens. They are in nursing school and their exams are tomorrow; they tell me they want to meditate to relieve their stress. They want the Koi ponds, tropical landscape and the shaded benches.

I point them to the gate across the street. But as the conversation unfolds I am surprisingly able to share with them the peace that comes through Jesus. I let them know, in atypical fashion, that I am a pastor and would love to teach them how to pray to Jesus and meditate in a way that will relieve their stress. They kindly thank me, but let me know that it is not Jesus or the church they need, just meditation in the gardens. Once more Wholly Jesus is not on the radar when people seek wholeness.

In order to enter into the conversation on wholeness, believers and pastors alike must become convinced about the role of the church in the world—salt and light. Pastors are the gatekeepers. Our involvement in wholeness can't simply be a clever, evangelistic baiting technique to win souls. We must truly believe that transformation of all things is a part of our message, as it was for Wholly Jesus. Our theologians, medical and nutritional professionals, ethicists, therapists, judges and trainers need the encouragement that what they do is part of something greater, part of the coming kingdom. We must view salvation as it was originally—that of saving the whole person without losing or compromising the truth of the forgiveness of sins.

A Wholly Jesus is not a new Jesus. It is a return to the king of the kingdom. It is a return to a seamless Gospel that is in the streets and not primarily in buildings. It is a return to a multidimensional Gospel that enters into all facets of life rather than a reductionistic, linear Gospel that only focuses on a commitment prayer. It is a return to a Gospel that invades culture rather than retreats from culture. It is turning from the shrunken, thin Jesus, to the bold, Ancient of Days who makes all things new. It is the recapturing of the radical Jesus with a huge, all-encompassing message that changes everything. His approach was holistic with the restoration of a person's relationship with the Father at the core. We must return to our evangelical roots, bringing wholeness and salvation back together.

The church must get off the defense and boldly enter the cultural arenas. We must see ourselves as the carrier of the torch of justice, ecology and human wholeness. We can no longer afford to be a separated church from society, protecting her doctrine or merely waiting for the rapture. The great cultural need is for a church without walls, fearlessly reaching out to a broken world with a holistic message of healing. A church that encourages its people to leave the locker room of the sanctuary to play the game on the field of everyday life. A church that is encouraged to enter and travel every stream of culture as salt and light to the world.

We must allow science to play its rightful role in determining the efficacy of various techniques, medicines and remedies of wholeness. Anecdotal information must not be the final word, nor can "Christian" be enough. We can't be the defenders of truth and then lower our standards for some other aspect of a person's wholeness. If the effectiveness of a product or therapy is only anecdotal, we must be honest and say so.

And we must always let others know our source of knowledge. The problem with integration is always blurring the line between the truth and therapeutic techniques. They are not the same and techniques will change while the truth will not.

We must pray for the sick without being weird. In praying for the sick, part of the church's early mandate, we must be faithful but clear. We must faithfully pray in the context that is appropriate to each unique church, while staying clear of malpractice or poor theology. This may be regularly practiced in a service, among the pastors and elders, during the Lord's Supper or on special occasions or in a healing room. However, we must be cautious of presumptuous approaches to healing that require the healed to "claim" their healing.

Our deeds and message must match. We must learn to not simply be big on theory but big in practice. We must take a leading role in every aspect of wholeness if we truly value humans, this planet and the God who made it all. It must be the church at the forefront of caring for the sick, raising up healthcare practitioners, carrying out justice, defending the poor around the world and practicing green living.

All that we do must reflect the character of Wholly Jesus—the image of God. We must build churches without walls, true to the kingdom mission. We must also break away from reductionism and return to the ancient mandate to be salt and light. The church must learn to love tangibly and convey its desire to save all human beings in every stage of life. It must learn to be conversant in pluralistic society where many religions, therapies and techniques exist. It must understand that 90% of what we do is pre-evangelistic and equal in value to evangelism. We must be worshippers when we are on the street.

We must become better at dialoguing with people living in a pluralistic and syncretistic society. This world must know what believers think about truth, judgment and love, and how these play out on the stage of life with people of other faiths, other races, other sexual preferences, other political beliefs, and other socio-economic backgrounds. We must learn to rejoice with them in their longing for love, justice and truth, and then build trust and keep the dialogue going. We must abandon our mono-logical ways, the darn-right warring attitudes, the protectionist suburban stance and enter a culture already bent toward wholeness. Wholly Jesus is already there; now we must join him.

The church has an unprecedented opportunity to return to the ancient, holistic gospel of Jesus Christ that knows no redemptive bounds. All we must do is become his hands and feet on this planet and in our sphere of influence. In the story of the paralytic, it was his friends, carrying the stretcher, who were the true heroes. They just knew that if they could get their friend to Jesus, he would take care of the rest. They made every effort to get their friend to Jesus hoping for his healing. But what the paralytic received was a healing and more—the forgiveness of sins. We must be these determined friends, bringing a broken world to Wholly Jesus.

***

Once more, I sit drinking coffee at Swami's, pecking away on my keyboard. I already had my walk on the beach, but the Garden was locked so here I sit. I am surrounded by people, some eating a healthy bowl of Acai while others down some greasy potatoes. This is the world in which I live and the world into which I must bring a unique message.

Ours is an alien wholeness—a remedy for wholeness different than any other. Wholly Jesus does have a word to speak in this holistic, pluralistic, ecological, peace-seeking world. And his message of transformed people transforming their world is radically unique and wonderfully freeing.

The criticalness of the hour is obvious. The wholeness movement is sweeping the Western world together with a desire for social reform and ecological preservation of our planet. And although many believers have entered into the dialogue, they are the minority. I have always maintained that Christians have the Wholly Grail. They have an integrated roadmap regarding all of these issues being discussed and dissected, and it is found in the redemption Jesus offered 2,000 years ago.

What the prophets foretold, what the disciples beheld and what many more for many years proclaimed, was a transformation that penetrates all of life. Each of these people ultimately understood, as did Julian of Norwich, "All will be well." Wholeness will prevail.

In a world crying out for wholeness, we are the wholly messengers and this is our wholly message.

NOTES

CHAPTER 1: THE WHOLE WORLD HAS GONE WHOLE

1. Yogananda, Paramahansa, *The Autobiography of a Yogi*, Self-Realization Fellowship, 1946.
2. According to a market study titled "Yoga in America" conducted in 2006 by the industry's foremost authority, the *Yoga Journal*, www.yogajournal.com.
3. According to an online article in the American Medical Association's newspaper American Medical News found here: http://www.ama-assn.org/amed-news/2002/10/28/prsa1028.htm

CHAPTER 2: OLD CHEWING GUM

1. Rhodes, Phillip, *An Outline History of Medicine*, Butterworth-Heinemann, 1985.
2. Ibid.
3. Ibid.
4. Ibid.
5. Kittel, Gerhard, Friedrich, Gerhard, transl. Bromiley, Geoffrey, *Theological Dictionary of the NT*, Abridged, 1985.

CHAPTER 3: PIRATES, MUTINY AND MUTATION

1. Rayl, A. J. S., *The High Price of a Broken Heart*, Psychology Today, Jul/Aug, 07.
2. Lewis, C. S., *The Weight of Glory and Other Addresses*, pp 3-4, 1941.
3. Loder, James, *The Transforming Moment*, Helmers and Howard, 2 ed., 1989.
4. Anderson, Ray, *On Being Human*, Fuller Seminary Press, 1982, p. 88.

CHAPTER 4: BROKEN MASTERPIECES

1. Lewis, C. S., *Mere Christianity* , Macmillan, 1977, pp. 106.
2. Lewis, C. S., *The Weight of Glory*.
3. Thielicke, Helmut, *Being Human—Becoming Human*, Doubleday, 1984.
4. Lewis, C. S., *The Weight of Glory*.
5. Lewis, C. S., *Mere Christianity*, p. 39.
6. May, Gerald, *Will and Spirit*, HarperOne, 1987.
7. Loder, James, Ibid.
8. Foreman, Jon, "Economy of Mercy," *Learning to Breathe*. Sparrow Records, 2000

CHAPTER 5: THE INVASION HAS BEGUN

1. Niebuhr, Richard, *Christ and Culture*, Harper and Row, 1956.
2. Ibid.
3. Ibid.
4. Ibid.
5. Willard, Dallas, *Divine Conspiracy*, Harper San Francisco, 1988, p. 40.
6. Ortiz, Juan, *Disciple*, Creation House, 1977.

CHAPTER 6: WHOLLY JESUS IN A MATERIAL WORLD

1. Wright, N. T., *Surprised by Hope*, HarperOne, 2008.
2. Kelsey, Morton, *Healing and Christianity*, Harper and Row, 1st ed., 1976.
3. Ibid, 88-89.
4. Ibid, 98.
5. Ibid, 100.
6. Ibid.
7. Levin, Jeff, *God, Faith, and Health*, Wiley, 2002.
8. Kelsey, p. 99.

CHAPTER 7: MANGERS, MUSTARD SEEDS, CHILDREN AND CROSSES

1. Guinness, Os, *The Call*, Nelson, 2003.
2. Foreman, Jon, Switchfoot, "Sooner or Later", *New Way to be Human*, Rethink Records, EMI.

CHAPTER 8: THE WHOLLY TROJAN HORSE

1. Lewis, C. S., *Mere Christianity*, p. 31.
2. Ladd, George, *The Presence of the Future*, Eerdmans, 1974.
3. Ibid.
4. Philippians 1:6
4. Lewis, C. S., *Mere Christianity*, 36.

Chapter 9: Raising the Bar to Normal
1. Lewis, C. S., *Abolition of Man*, HarperOne, 2001
2. Green, Michael, *Evangelism in the Early Church*, Eerdmans, 2004.
3. Cho, Simon, *Spiritual Theology*, InterVarsity Press, 1998.

Chapter 10: Becoming Spirit People
1. Kinnaman, David and Lyons, Gabe, *Unchristian*. Baker Books, 2007.
2. Redman, Matt, "Heart of Worship", Survivor Records, 1999.
3. Bunyan, John, *Pilgrim's Progress*, Viking Press, 1959.
4. Dunn, James , *The Baptism of the Holy Spirit*, SCM Press, 1970.

Chapter 11: Risk, Sacrifice and Wholly Transformation
1. Niebuhr, Richard, Christ and Culture, Harper and Brothers, 1951
48. Enroth, Ron, *Churches That Abuse*, Zondervan, 1993; Blue, Ken, *Healing Spiritual Abuse*, InterVarsity Press, 1993; Arterburn, Stephen, and Felton, Jack, Toxic Faith, Shaw Books, 2001.

Chapter 13: Wholeness Will Prevail
1. APA PsychNET.
2. Avalos, Hector, *Health Care and the Rise of Christianity*, Hendrickson, 1999; Morton Kelsey, *Healing and Christianity*.
3. Erwin, Gayle, *Jesus Style*, Ronald Haynes, 1983.

WHAT NOW?

My hope is that this book stirs you to action instead of a simple head nod in agreement. So, where do we go from here? At the book's website - www.whollyjesus.com - I have listed the websites of organizations that I think would be beneficial for people to connect with as they seek to put the ideals from this book into practice. Also, please feel free to send your comments to me through the website.

- Mark Foreman

To personally dig deeper, or to take your group through an expanded learning experience of **Wholly Jesus**, register at the newest online learning system that is both fun and rich in training: Shapevine.com

Shapevine Learning Podules offer learners a peer-based learning community with video and interactive media tools that makes information become incarnation. Go to www.shapevine.com and click on "ELearning" and you can start today!